A. Y. Hubbell

Prominent men of Staten Island, 1893

A. Y. Hubbell

Prominent men of Staten Island, 1893

ISBN/EAN: 9783743322387

Manufactured in Europe, USA, Canada, Australia, Japa

Cover: Foto ©ninafisch / pixelio.de

Manufactured and distributed by brebook publishing software (www.brebook.com)

A. Y. Hubbell

Prominent men of Staten Island, 1893

PROMINENT MEN

OF

STATEN ISLAND

1893.

ALL RIGHTS RESERVED.

NEW YORK.
A. Y. HUBBELL, Publisher.
1893.

INDEX.

Name	Page	Name	Page
Acker, Augustus	51	Kreischer, Charles C.	71
Androvette, John M.	13	Kreischer, Edward B	73
Androvette, Peter	99	Langton, David M	52
Bacot, William S.	81	Latourette, Paul	48
Barger, James	112	Macormac, Samuel A	53
Bethel Church	133	Marsh, Isaac M	142
Bloom, Rev. Frederick	132	Marsh, Nathaniel	23
Bodine, Benjamin J	35	Minnahan, John E	54
Bowen, William	47	Morrison, Henry P	39
Brown, Benjamin	83	Muller, Edward M	13
Brown, Robert P	43	Mulligan, James E	26
Buel, Horace E	87	O'Grady, Joseph F	63
Byrnes, Rev. James Patrick	136	Randolph, Rev. D. B. F	140
Casey, William C	56	Rinscher, Frank	97
Cole, Abram	25	Roehre, Dr. R	95
Coleman, David M., M. D.	120	Schaefer, George T	37
Collins, Michael J	64	Seguine, Crowell M	127
Conklin, Capt. Michael	93	Shea, Cornelius	113
Corbett, William W	91	Simonson, Cornelius	49
Dailey, John Linderman	79	Simonson, Reuben	130
Detrick, Calvin	89	Stake, Geo. W	112
Doyle, Hon. Edward P	75	Stephens, Hon. Stephen D	9
Egbert, George T	59	St. Patrick's Church	135
Elsworth, John H	77	St. Peter's Church	138
Feeny, John E., M. D.	29	Suydam, William A	107
Fetherston, John J	62	Tiernan, Peter	55
Finley, William	39	Totten, Ephraim J	117
Fisher, George W	51	Tully, Matthew S	17
Fitzgerald, Thomas W	15	Turner, John	101
Gannon, Frank S	69	Ulman, Percival Glenroy	111
Gauss, Rev. J. J	139	VanName, Calvin D	105
Golder, Robert Henry	119	Van Name, J. Howard	31
Griffin, Oliver H	45	Vaughan, John J, Jr	38
Hadkins, Frank L	129	Vitt, Franklin C	41
Hervey, Edwin Addison, M. D.	123	Warde, John S	85
Hoag, Orry Huested	125	Warford, Benjamin H	126
Hubbell, Charles Livingston	109	Whitman, Stephen E., M. D.	6112
Hughes, Martin	36	Widdecombe, John	115
Hull, Rev. C. F	137	Wood, Dr. J. Walter, A. M., M. D.	121
Johnstone, Louis Morris	57	Wyeth Charles	103
Kenney, John J	19	Wyeth, Nathaniel Jarvis	143
Kenny, Thomas, Jr	40	Yetman, Hon. Hubbard R	21
Kerr, James	61	Young, J. L	146
Kreischer, B	67		

INDEX TO SUPPLEMENT.

Abrams, Andrew	160		Manee, E. Stewart	189
Atlantic Inn	174		Marshall, Walter	206
Ayres, M. C.	177		McCabe, James	210
Ayres, M. C. (Deceased)	178		McGuire, Michael	153
Brown, Philip J.	190		Moore, T. W., Jr	162
Browne, Wm. J.	157		Mord's Drygoods Emporium	167
Butler, D. C.	196		Newhall, John B.	152
Butler, David J.	181		Pollock, R. W.	149
Butler, Israel, Jr	180		Schaefer, Edmund G.	165
Cleveland, H. E.	188		Seaton, James	156
Cleveland, Wilson A.	164		Seguine, C. M. (residence)	207
Egbert, Geo. L.	198		Sharrett, Horatio J.	163
Ellis, George W.	155		Shea, Cornelius A.	166
Ellis, Hampton C.	183		Simonson, S. D., & Co.	205
Ellis, Jacob S.	182		Slaight, Elmer E.	161
Floersch, Peter	192		Slover, Stephen H.	171
Foster, James	209		Snedeker, Livingston, Jr	172
Furman, John T.	193		Stephen's House	170
Herrel, Jacob	187		Streeter, Benj. E.	159
Hoyer, Charles E.	154		Totten, W. H.	204
Kadletz, K.	208		Tysen, William	201
Keeley, James D.	179		Vaughn, John G.	150
Kennedy, Dr. S. J.	200		Vere, Howard M., D. D. S.	186
Kessler, Hugo	158		Wilbur, Charles F.	168
Killmeyer, Nicholas	194		Wilkins, Fred	176
LaForge, James	202		Wood, John B.	184
Manee, Charles C.	169			

OFFICIAL.

HON. STEPHEN D. STEPHENS.

STEPHEN DOVER STEPHENS, the county judge and surrogate of Richmond county, was born beneath the shadow of the court-house at Richmond on the 19th day of April, 1845. His father and paternal ancestors for three generations back were born in New York city, his mother and maternal ancestors being natives of Staten Island. Judge Stephens pursued his preparatory studies at Trinity School, New York city, subsequently passed with honor through the several departments of Columbia College, and in 1866 he was graduated from that institution with the degree of Bachelor of Arts. Subsequently he entered Columbia College Law School, and in 1868 was graduated therefrom with the degree of Bachelor of Laws. In the following year he received the degree of Master of Arts. He immediately entered upon the practice of the law and continued in active practice until he was elevated to his present position.

In politics, Judge Stephens is a Democrat. In 1873, he was elected to represent Richmond county in the Assembly of 1874, and served on the important committee on railroads and also that of villages. In 1874, he was again elected to represent the county in the Assembly of 1875, and that year served as chairman of the committee on villages and also as a member of the committee on railroads and public lands. In the "Life Sketches" of 1875, we find this said of him: "Mr. Stephens is an active and energetic young man and represents the county of Richmond for the second time. He is a finely educated gentleman, a good public speaker, and, owing to his industrious habits and executive ability, is exceedingly valuable in the details of legislation and committee work."

In 1881, Mr. Stephens was elected to his present position over Tompkins Westervelt, the Republican candidate, by a handsome majority; and in 1887, he was re-elected, practically without opposition, the Republicans making no nomination against him. During

HON. STEPHEN D. STEPHENS,
County Judge and Surrogate.

his twelve years of service as county judge and surrogate, some of the most important cases which have ever arisen in Richmond county have been before him. Rarely has an appeal from his decisions been taken, and never has he been reversed by the court of last resort, the court of appeals.

He is a member of the Episcopal denomination and is a regular attendant at old St. Andrew's, at Richmond, in which church he was brought up, and where his ancestors worshipped before him.

In 1884, Judge Stephens married Agnes L. Lasar, of Brooklyn, a descendant of the old Pitkin family of Connecticut. The union has proved a most happy one and two sons have been born to them, viz: Stephen D., Junior, and Richmond, the latter having been named after the county and the place of Judge Stephens' birth, for which he has always maintained the greatest affection.

Happy in his domestic life, with an unsullied family history and with an unimpeachable record of his own, both in private and public life, Judge Stephens may well be classed as one of the most prominent men in Richmond county.

EDWARD M. MULLER,
Sheriff of Richmond County.

EDWARD M. MULLER was born in the city of New York, Jan. 28th, 1864. His first school days were spent in old Grammar school No. 29, from which he was graduated with honors, and then entered the College of the City of New York, where he took a commercial course.

After leaving college, he at once received a responsible position in the service of the Delaware, Lackawanna and Western Railroad Company, and is now in business with his father as transportation agents.

Mr. Muller gained considerable prominence in school circles, during his boyhood days, on account of his ability to master his studies, and his talents which were then carefully cultivated and guarded, have indeed developed into rare business qualifications. He is a fine accountant, and ranks as an able mathematician. He has travelled considerably, and it is said in financial circles that he has handled as much money in his business career as any man of age in the great metropolis. Mr. Muller's knowledge of the railroads of this country is very large.

He was elected sheriff of Richmond county, as a Democrat, in 1891, and is the youngest sheriff that has ever been elected in the county of Richmond, and in fact in the state of New York. He has instituted many reforms in the sheriff's office, and has been repeatedly complimented by the judiciary and the grand jury on the efficient manner in which he has conducted his office.

Personally, Mr. Muller is a man whose friendship is valued by all who bear his acquaintance; cool and collected, but with a heart filled with warm impulses; with a mind clear and determined as to his line of duty; with a character above reproach and an integrity that no one will question; with pure intentions, and with the laudable ambition of doing right under all circumstances.

THOMAS W. FITZGERALD,
District-Attorney.

THOS. W. FITZGERALD was born in New York, September 1st, 1854. He was educated in the New York common schools and the College of the City of New York.

He entered the law office of the late Francis N. Bangs, November 1st, 1871, with whom he remained until January 16th, 1884.

In 1872, he moved to Staten Island, and has resided here ever since. He was admitted to the bar in 1875 and practised in the office where he studied until 1884, when he left to accept the position of clerk of the court of the city of New York, but still continued the practice of his profession. He was appointed by President Cleveland, a member of the board of pension appeals, in 1887.

In March 1889, he was appointed secretary of the board of police commissioners of Richmond county, a position which he held until January 1890, when he resigned to assume the duties of district-attorney, an office to which he had been elected the previous November, and to which he was re-elected in November 1892, by the largest majority ever given any person for that office. He will be a member of the Constitutional Convention to meet in Albany in May 1894. Among the important cases which he has tried and brought to a successful issue during his term of office are the following: People vs. Emmons, murder; People vs. Kinsella, manslaughter; People vs. Mahoney, arson and several others.

Mr. Fitzgerald has always been a Democrat, has been for many years a member of the Democratic county committee, and has often been elected delegate to the state conventions, and for the past three years has been vice-chairman of the Democratic General Committee. He has made quite a reputation in all parts of the state as a campaign speaker, and is well known in the county as an earnest and forcible advocate of the principles of his party.

MATTHEW S. TULLY,
County Treasurer.

No young man in Richmond county has been called upon to perform more responsible duties or has performed them with more credit to himself than County Treasurer Matthew S. Tully.

Mr. Tully, eldest son of the late County Treasurer James Tully, was born in New Brighton, Nov. 29th, 1865, and received a thorough education in the schools of the Island. At the early age of twenty-two he was appointed tax-receiver, and a few months later, on the death of his father, in February 1888, Mr. Tully being the eldest son, not only assumed charge of the large business left by his father, but was appointed county treasurer to serve out his father's unexpired term.

Before Mr. Tully's first term of office he had so fully demonstrated his ability and fitness for the office that he was made the regular Democratic nominee for re-election to the same office; and was the only candidate on the ticket who was elected. His campaign was a model one, being entirely free from "mud slinging."

Mr. Tully instituted a new system of handling the public moneys, whereby he can at any time, within a few moments, ascertain the exact financial condition of the county. He also arranged a list of back taxes which greatly facilitated their collector and brought over $40,000 into the treasury. His business methods so pleased the board of supervisors, that, after auditing his accounts in 1890, they adopted a resolution complimenting him on his system of keeping the accounts of the office, and the correctness of his books.

In 1891, he was again given the Democratic nomination without opposition and easily won the victory over his opponent.

Very few persons are aware of the amount of money passing through this office. During the past seven years it has amounted to about $2,500,000, the receipts of taxes and road money, are nearly $400,000 annually, and so carefully have the books been kept that they show where every penny of this large amount has gone and for what it has been expended.

Mr. Tully has been as successful in his private business relations as in his official career.

JOHN J. KENNEY,
School Commissioner.

JOHN J KENNEY, the eldest son of Patrick and Mary Kenney, was born in New York city, March 2nd, 1858. He removed with his family to Staten Island, when six weeks old, and has ever since resided here. He was educated in the best public schools of the county, taking a high rank from the first, as a quick and intelligent student. After graduating, he began life as a teacher in the Madison avenue public school, in New Brighton, and taught for nearly three years. He then entered the law office of the late Tompkins Westervelt, county judge of Richmond county; was admitted to the bar at Brooklyn, Feb. 12th, 1880, after which he established an office in New Brighton, Staten Island, and has since enjoyed a lucrative practice.

In July 1882, he was elected clerk of the village of New Brighton, which position he filled with entire satisfaction to the board of trustees for nine years. He resigned July 25th, 1891, in order to give more attention to the practice of the law.

He was elected school commissioner of Richmond County in Nov. 1887, and administered the office with such entire satisfaction to the public that he was re-elected in 1890, receiving the largest majority of any candidate on the ticket.

He has been especially devoted and energetic in the performance of his duties as school commissioner. Under his supervision there has been a constant improvement in the government and management of schools. He inaugurated in this county, the system of uniform examination for teachers' licenses, which has resulted in producing a better class of teachers, and abolished the system by which licenses were issued as a favor and frequently with the merest pretense of examination. School buildings have received his attention to the extent of securing new buildings of modern design and great value. His vigorous work secured new buildings at Port Richmond, West Brighton, Graniteville, Garretsons, Giffords, New Springville and Richmond.

In spite of Mr. Kenney's popularity with all classes, he still remains unmarried.

HUBBARD R. YETMAN,
Member of Assembly.

The Hon. Hubbard R. Yetman was born in Monmouth county, New Jersey, in 1847, and was educated in the high school at Freehold. When scarcely fifteen years of age he enlisted in the 14th Regt. N. Y. Vols., and went to the front as drummer boy. He remained until his regiment was mustered out at the close of the war, and was in a number of severe engagements. He, however, escaped without any serious injury. On his return from the army he settled at Tottenville, and taught in the public schools for fifteen years. During this time he was elected to the office of justice of the peace for several terms and also represented several insurance companies for which he secured a large business.

In 1888, he received the Democratic nomination of member of assembly and was elected by a heavy majority. He was again elected to the assembly in 1891 and 1892, in both instances receiving large majorities. During each of Mr. Yetman's terms in the assembly he was honored by important committee appointments.

Among the important laws passed during Mr. Yetman's three terms as a member of the legislature, affecting Richmond county, were the following:

To settle the boundary line in the Kill von Kull, between the states of New York and New Jersey.

To establish a board of county assessors.

To establish a board of county excise commissioners.

To change the senatorial and congressional districts.

To tax the property known as Sailors' Snug Harbor.

To amend the laws relating to water supply for villages.

To extend the terms of supervisors to two years and fix the salary at $1,000 per year.

To extend the term of police commissioners to five years.

To increase the police force of the county.

To cede to the United States property adjoining Fort Wadsworth.

To create a fund for pensioning retired police officers.

Mr. Yetman was married, in 1870, to Miss Sarah Joline, of Tottenville, and has four children: **Laura, Arthur, Grace** and **Willie.**

NATHANIEL MARSH,
Supervisor for Southfield and Chairman of the Board.

NATHANIEL MARSH, the eldest son of the late Nathaniel Marsh, a former president of the Erie railroad, was born and reared in the Marsh homestead, at Clifton, one of the most stately houses on the hills overlooking New York bay. He is a graduate of Princeton College and of Columbia Law School, head of the law firm of Marsh & Bull, 19 Broadway, New York city, and has been for several years counsel to the board of health.

His first official position was that of trustee from the Southfield ward of the village of Edgewater, and largely through his efforts the village debt, amounting to $100,000, was paid off and the credit of the village raised to the highest point.

During his term as supervisor for his town, he has seen the interest on the bonded indebtedness descend from seven per cent., with bonds at a discount, to three or three and a half per cent. and selling at the premium—a change that has been wrought largely through his excellent financial ability.

Mr. Marsh is now serving his fourteenth consecutive year as supervisor of the town of Southfield, and for thirteen years of this time he has been unanimously chosen by his associates in the board as their chairman, a record which is probably unequaled by any man in the state of New York. During his long connection with the board of supervisors, Mr. Marsh has rarely missed a meeting except when absent from the county. More than any other man connected with the board, Mr. Marsh has given his time and talent to carry on the business incident to his position and to carry out the many improvements and reforms connected with the affairs of our county. The success of the new county road law, and the construction of nearly thirty miles of the finest roads have been largely due to the untiring efforts of Mr. Marsh.

Mr. Marsh has also, since June 1889, been the police magistrate of the village of Edgewater, a position which he has filled to the great satisfaction of all law abiding citizens, and the gratifying decrease of crime in the community is largely due to the manner in which Mr. Marsh has conducted this important office.

In addition to these public offices, Mr. Marsh is one of the oldest directors of the Staten Island Railway, a director and member of the executive committee of the Richmond County Gas Light Company, of which corporation he is likewise counsel, is one of the original members of the Staten Island Cricket and Base Ball Club, and is now the president of the Clifton Boat Club, vice-president of the Clifton Tennis Club, and a member of the S. I. Athletic Club.

ABRAM COLE,
Supervisor for Westfield.

ABRAM COLE comes of a long line of Staten Island ancestors, his great-great-grandfather, Isaac Cole, having been one of the early settlers on the Island and the owner of a large tract of land at Prince's Bay. Mr. Cole was born in 1856 and is the fourth generation of his family bearing the name of Abram, and is the manager of the large lumber and coal business, established by his father in 1857, near Tottenville, at what is known as Weir's Mills.

At the death of Mr. Cole's father which occurred in September 1876, the business descended to his sons and is now carried on under the firm name of Cole Bros., the members of which, beside Mr. Cole, are his brothers, Jacob W. and James T.

Mr. Cole was educated in the public school of Tottenville, after which he took a course of study at the Polytechnic Institute in Brooklyn. He has always been an active Republican, and, although never courting office, has been, by the urgency of his party, kept almost continuously in office for the past nine years, having been three times elected to the office of town clerk and for six successive years elected to the office of supervisor, which office he still holds, of a town almost uniformly polling a Democratic vote at state elections.

When Mr. Cole began his first term as supervisor he was the youngest supervisor who ever represented his town, and he has held the office for more consecutive years than any other man during the present generation. He is now, next to Supervisor Marsh, the senior member of the board, in length of service. From the fact that ever since Mr. Cole has been in the board of supervisors he has been the only Republican in the board he has acquired the title of the "lone star."

Mr. Cole's strength lies not so much in his politics as in the fact that he always brings to bear on questions of public policy the same sound principles that he applies to his own business.

Mr. Cole has often been earnestly urged by his party to accept the nomination for the more important county offices and for member of assembly, believing that his popularity and well-known ability and integrity would enable the party to overcome the large Democratic majority, but he has uniformly refused the most tempting offers.

Mr. Cole was married in 1880 to Blanche, only daughter of Capt. Abel Martin, of Tottenville, by whom he has two sons, Ralph M., aged 10 years, and Chester A., aged 12 years.

JAMES E. MULLIGAN,
Supervisor for Castleton.

JAMES E. MULLIGAN, eldest son of the late Edward Mulligan, was born in Columbia county in 1845. Soon after his birth, the family moved to Troy, N. Y., his father having been appointed assistant to the superintendent of the New York Central and Hudson River Railroad.

In 1853, the family moved to Staten Island, where James, then a lad of eight, was sent to the New Brighton public school, the same school of which he was afterward trustee for seventeen years.

In 1874, he formed a co-partnership with his present partner, Paul F. Brazo, in the painting, decorating and paper-hanging business. In 1881, the firm established a store at Long Branch, N. J., where it is doing perhaps the largest business of the kind in the state, giving employment to from sixty to seventy men. It has also a third store at Sea Bright, N. J.

The firm has always been known for its energy and "push," for artistic taste in selecting goods, for promptness in executing orders, and excellent and thorough manner of doing its work.

Mr. Mulligan was a member of the second excise board ever elected in the town of Castleton. He was a strenuous high license man, but, owing to the fact that the other members of the board were less progressive in their ideas, he was unable to affect any reform, and refused re-election.

In 1890, he was appointed a member of the board of health, of the village of Castleton, and made one of the most efficient presidents the board ever had.

On the resignation in 1892, of Robert Moore, who had held the office of supervisor of the town of Castleton for many years, Mr. Mulligan was appointed to fill the vacancy, and, at the expiration of the term, he was re-elected for the term of two years.

On his appointment to fill the unexpired term of Mr. Moore, the Richmond County *Herald* said:

"Mr. Mulligan's broadmindedness, upon matters affecting the welfare of all classes, together with his sterling business capacity and exquisite tact, render him an extremely proper and fitting person to safeguard and promote the general interests of the town in which he has lived so long, and which has conferred upon him the distinguished honor of supervisorship. With him that honor will remain intact and unsullied."

The above prediction has been amply fulfilled.

JOHN L. FEENY,
Supervisor for Middletown.

JOHN L. FEENY, M. D., is the second oldest son of the late Dr. Joseph Feeny, of Stapleton, who opened in 1849, the first drug store established on Staten Island, and who was one of the leading physicians on the Island in the early sixties. He afterward moved to Jersey City, where his reputation as a successful physician had evidently preceded him, as he was made health officer of the city the next year after taking up his residence there. Dr. Joseph Feeny was one of the most scholarly men of the county, and before he began the practice of his profession was the principal of one of the most thorough classical institutes ever established on the Island. He died at his residence in Jersey City in 1866.

Dr. John L. Feeny was from his earliest boyhood selected by his father as his successor in the medical profession. At the early age of fifteen years he had acquired an excellent classical education and began the study of medicine under the late Dr. Thos. C. Moffatt, at the same time getting a large practical experience at the Seamen's Retreat Hospital, where he remained until he entered the University of New York Medical Department, from which he was graduated in 1866 among the highest in the class. During his college course he studied under such famous physicians as Valentine Mott, Alfred C. Post, William H. VanBuren, Alfred Loomis and John T. Metcalfe; also under Professors Budd, Paine and the Drapers. After leaving the university he took a special and private course under Professor Ayelette. It will be seen, therefore, that his father, being a prominent physician himself, was able to secure as instructors for his son, the most famous physicians and teachers of that day.

Upon completing his course of study, he was appointed house physician to the "Seamen's Retreat," a position which he filled with honor until 1869, when he resigned to enter on private practice in Stapleton. In 1870, he was appointed physician to the metropolitan police, and is now surgeon to the Richmond county police, has been health officer for the town of Middletown and the village of Edgewater for many years, and is a member of the Richmond County Medical Society.

The thorough instruction which Dr. Feeny received under the distinguished physicians at the University enabled him to take a high rank in his profession, and to be especially sought for consultation in intricate cases. He has had, from the first, a practice second to none in the county, and his success with difficult cases has given him the confidence of the entire community.

In the spring of 1893, Dr. Feeny was elected to the board of supervisors and immediately began one of the most searching and thorough examinations into the finances of the county which has been made for many years, and while the investigation is not yet completed, enough has been established to prove that the county will greatly profit by the doctor's services.

In private life the doctor is one of the most congenial and companionable of men and has a host of devoted friends. In his professional and official duties whatever he has to do is done thoroughly and well, not the smallest details being overlooked or omitted.

Of Dr. Feeny, Prestons History of Staten Island, published in 1886, says:

"Dr. Feeny has now been in active practice more than sixteen years, during which time many remarkable cases have come under his notice and been treated by him. He adds to his large experience an intense love not only of his profession but of all scientific and artistic study. He is up in the classics, has traveled considerably, and has taken a deep interest in historical research. His cordial manners and general intelligence have long been noticed by those who enjoy his acquaintance, and have resulted in endearing him to them."

"The deep interest which he has taken in the health of the community in which he lives, and the county at large and especially the freedom with which he responded to a call made on him for lectures on hygienic subjects during the recent cholera agitation will long be remembered with pleasure by the people of Staten Island."

And we may add that no physician on the Island took a more active part in suppressing the smallpox, which came near becoming epidemic on the Island a few years ago.

Dr. Feeny was married June 9, 1870, to Miss Emma Bateman, daughter of the famous engineer, John F. Bateman, of Maine. They have four children living, Mildred, Marguerite, Elsa and John L. Jr.

SUPERVISOR VAN NAME.

JOSEPH HOWARD VANNAME, present supervisor of the town of Northfield, comes of a long line of Staten Island ancestors, who have been prominent in business for nearly two centuries.

Mr. Van Name is the eldest son of the late Charles Van Name, and was born March 27th, 1835. His father was a merchant for nearly half a century. When he retired from active life the business was continued by his two sons, Joseph H. and George W.

Mr. Van Name is a Democrat, but is better known as a business man than a politician, although he has several times been called by his neighbors to fill public offices. He has served several terms as town clerk of the town of Northfield, and in 1891 was elected to the office of supervisor which office he has since filled to the entire satisfaction of his constituents.

In 1856, Mr. Van Name married Caroline, the youngest daughter of the late Thomas Gibson. They have one son, George.

HENRY P. MORRISON,
County Engineer of Roads.

HENRY PRENTICE MORRISON was born in Troy, N. Y., on January 14th, 1858.

His early education consisted of a course in the public schools of New York city, from which he was graduated in 1873. From here he went to Clark's Academy, graduating in 1876, when he entered the University of the City of New York as a freshman, graduating in 1880 and having two degrees conferred on him, namely, Bachelor of Science and Civil Engineer. While an under-graduate of the University he was twice president of the Philomatheon Society, a member of the Psi-Upsilon Fraternity and was selected by the faculty to represent the University in oratory at the inter-collegiate contest of 1880, receiving second award at the contest, there being ten colleges represented.

After his graduation from the University Mr. Morrison received a position with John S. Bogert, then secretary of the American Society of Civil Engineers, as secretary to that gentleman. His health being poor he sought active field work and secured an engagement on the Eastern Shore railroad of Maryland and there remained until he was appointed to the department of public works in New York city, being assigned to the bureau of sewers. He followed sewerage engineering for eighteen months and was then promoted and transferred to the paving department, becoming first assistant to Horace Loomis, then engineer in charge of paving in New York city. For the past eleven years he has made a specialty of paving and road building, refusing all offers of transfer to other departments, in many cases valuable, in order that he might stay at his specialty, and has planned, estimated for, and performed the engineering work on over six million dollars' worth of pavement of all classes, an experience in that line such as few engineers in the United States have had. He has also built up a large private clientage, among whom are some of the heaviest quarry and iron contractors in the country.

In the spring of 1893, Mr. Morrison was appointed county road engineer of Richmond county. Although he has held this office but a few months the evidence of his skill in road building is seen in every part of the county.

It is safe to say that Richmond county has no more industrious or competent official than Road Engineer Morrison.

Mr. Morrison, when not engaged in his professional duties, devotes his time to his family, a wife and two daughters, Edna Belle, two and one-half years old, and Ruth Von Eiff, four months old, "papa's boys" as they are affectionately termed.

BENJAMIN J. BODINE,
Superintendent of the County Poor.

BENJAMIN J. BODINE was born Jan. 7th, 1849, at Castleton Corners. His father, Abram Bodine, was one of the 1849 pioneers to the California gold regions.

Mr. Bodine was educated in the schools of Staten Island. When only fourteen years of age he ran away from home and enlisted in the Union Army joining Battery C., 3rd U. S. Artillery, Regulars, then stationed in the Shenandoah Valley, Captain D. R. Ransom commanding. He served in the Army of the Potomac under Gen. Hancock, taking part in many of the important battles fought along the Potomac and around Richmond. After the close of the war he was sent to the Platte Valley, Neb., where he served in the Indian war until after the surrender of Spotted Tail. He was mustered out in 1866, when he returned to Staten Island.

In 1868, he entered into co-partnership with Mr. John Smith, of Long Island, and carried on a fruit commission business at Norwalk, Conn. In 1872, he dissolved partnership with Mr. Smith and took the position of head salesman for Davis & Mayo, Hoboken, N. J., ship chandlers.

In 1876, he entered into partnership with Geo. W. Thackery, and again engaged in the fruit and vegetable business, running a sloop between New York, Elizabethport and Port Johnson. He remained in this business, doing a thriving trade, for nine years, until the death of Mr. Isaac Van Name, in 1885, made an opening for him to enter upon a prosperous grocery trade in the thriving village of Mariners' Harbor, as the manager of his son and successor, Oscar Van Name, where he remained until his appointment, in 1890, to the office of superintendent of the poor, which position he still holds.

A visit to this well-kept institution will show that Mr. Bodine's military training in the United States Regular Army has made him a model superintendent for a large institution, such as our county almshouse, and our board of supervisors have set the seal of their approval on his management not only with their "well done good and faithful servant," but have supplemented their words of praise by a liberal increase of salary.

There was probably no man better fitted for the position of superintendent of the almshouse than Mr. Bodine. His long experience in business had made him thoroughly acquainted with the value of provisions and the cost of supplies; and since he has been superintendent there has been no complaint of favoritism in the purchase of goods either in price or quality, but all the affairs of the almshouse have been managed after careful business methods by an experienced business man.

CORONER HUGHES.

MARTIN HUGHES, second son of Robert Hughes, was born in New York in 1857, and was educated at the Brothers' school and at St. Francis Xavier's College, after which he spent considerable time in the study of medicine. In 1871, he came, with his father's family, to Staten Island, where he has resided ever since. In 1885, he opened an undertaking office in Clifton, and he has built up a large and successful business.

In 1886, he was elected coroner on the Democratic ticket, and at the expiration of his term, was re-elected, and again in 1892, making three consecutive terms. Among the important cases which he has investigated as coroner, were the death of Miss Mary Tobin, the mystery of which no skill has been able to solve; the Emmons murder case, which resulted in the conviction of the murderer; the Crooke's crossing railroad accident, in which three persons were killed, and many other important cases which attracted much public attention at the time.

Coroner Hughes' knowledge of medicine, gained in early life, has proved a useful training, and enabled him to conduct difficult cases to a successful issue.

CORONER SCHAEFER.

GEORGE T. SCHAEFER, the eldest of fourteen children of Carl F. Schaefer, was born in New York city in 1853. He came to Staten Island with his father's family in 1859, and was educated in the public schools, with a year's course in the German school.

When thirteen years of age, he entered his father's shop to learn the trade of carpenter, cabinet-maker and upholsterer. Having thoroughly learned all branches of the trade, he started in business for himself at the age of twenty-two years, establishing the business of undertaker and embalmer, which he still conducts at 174 Bay st., Stapleton. In 1889, Mr. Schaefer was elected coroner for Richmond county, an office which he still holds, having been re-elected in 1892. During his term, he has conducted many important inquests and has made for himself an excellent record as a thorough and careful official.

UNDER-SHERIFF JOHN J. VAUGHAN, JR.

JOHN J. VAUGHAN, JR., was born in Wales in 1848. When he was eight years of age his parents moved to Rossville, Staten Island. At the age of fifteen years he enlisted in the Union Army, in Regt. 155 N. Y. Vols. of Corcoran's Irish Legion, which was then stationed at Camp Scott, and was assigned to duty as drummer.

He participated in the battles of Deserted Farms, Suffolk, Black Water, Eatonton Road, Spottsylvania Court House, Mattapony, North Anna, South Anna, Cold Harbor; assaults on Petersburg, June 16th, 17th, 18th and 22nd, 1864; Ream's Station, Hatcher's Run, Deep Bottom; the breaking of the Confederate lines in front of Petersburg, April 2nd, 1865; Burksville, and at High Bridge, where he was captured, three days before the surrender of General Lee at Appomattox. He was with Lee's army at the time of the surrender.

Since the close of the war Mr. Vaughan has held the office of under-sheriff two terms beside the present one, and the office of superintendent of the poor and of sheriff of Richmond county. He is also vice-senior past commander of Lenhart Post No. 163, G. A. R., and past chancellor of Richmond Lodge No. 80, K. of P.

SURROGATE'S CLERK FINLEY.

WILLIAM FINLEY, clerk to the surrogate's court of Richmond county, was born Oct. 19th, 1854, at Stapleton.

He is the eldest son of the late Michael Finley, who for over twenty years was manager of Mr. John Scott's livery stable at Clifton.

The subject of the above sketch received his education at the Broad street school, Stapleton, and in early life was employed as clerk by the firm of Armstrong & Frost.

His first public office was that of town auditor of the town of Southfield to which he was elected for two terms, and in 1878, 1879 and 1880 was elected tax collector of the same town.

On Jan. 1st, 1882, he was appointed by the Hon. Stephen D. Stephens, clerk to the surrogate's court, and was re-appointed Jan. 1st, 1888.

Mr. Finley was married Nov. 29th, 1883, to Eleanor S., daughter of Justice John L. Young, of Richmond, where he now resides with his wife and three children, Susie M., Margaret and Eleanor.

THOMAS KENNY, JR.

THOMAS KENNY, JR., eldest son of ex-revenue collector Thomas Kenny, of West New Brighton, was born at West New Brighton in 1866. He was educated in the Christian Brothers' School, of New York city, and the De La Salle Institute. After graduating from the Institute he completed a course in Walworth's Stenographic College, New York, where he had one of the most thorough masters and teachers in the profession. Immediately after receiving his diploma he was appointed by the Hon. Stephen D. Stephens as the official stenographer of the surrogate's court and county court and court of sessions, which position he still holds. He has the honor of being the youngest court stenographer in the state, and young as he is, he is rated as one of the leading, most careful and correct men in his profession.

Mr. Kenny is also president of the Young Men's Catholic Union, of West New Brighton, a position he has held with entire satisfaction to the members of the Union for the past seven years.

He is still unmarried and lives with his parents at West New Brighton, the place of his birth.

FRANKLIN C. VITT.

FRANKLIN C. VITT was born in New York city, May 1853. In 1865, his parents moved to Stapleton, where he completed his education at the public school.

In 1869, he secured a position with a law firm in New York, and his energy and natural ability soon raised him to the position of managing clerk, a position he held until the dissolution of the firm in 1876.

He was one of the promoters and founders of the famous Middletown "Boys in White," a Democratic club which has been a conspicuous feature in every Democratic campaign since its organization.

Mr. Vitt entered politics when quite a young man, and has always wielded a considerable influence in the councils of his, (the Democratic) party, and has often been elected to county and congressional conventions.

In 1883, he was elected justice to fill a vacancy, and in 1885 and again in 1889 and 1893, was re-elected for full terms.

In December 1890, Mr. Vitt was appointed clerk of the board of supervisors, a position which he still holds, and the duties of which office he has performed with such promptness, accuracy and fidelity, as to earn for him the reputation of being the best clerk the board of supervisors ever had.

POSTMASTER BROWN.

Robert P. Brown, postmaster of West New Brighton, N.Y., was born in Rahway, N. J., on Dec. 31st, 1844, and, when sixteen years of age, became a resident of Staten Island.

In 1862, he enlisted in Company C, 30th Regiment N. J. Volunteers, and, after serving continuously through his term of enlistment, was honorably discharged, and he returned to Staten Island, where he was engaged in business pursuits until May 1882, when he received his appointment to his present position of postmaster from President Chester A. Arthur.

Mr. Brown performed his official duties with such conscientious zeal, efficiency and courtesy, that he not only won the respect and warm regard of all, but with an increase of more than one-third in the population the business of his office has been quadrupled under his vigorous administration and the office promoted from the third to the second class, and, on July 1st, 1890, it was made a free delivery office.

The efficiency and zeal of Mr. Brown were made known by his best patrons of both parties to President Cleveland, who retained him in office through his first administration, and to President Harrison, by whom he was re-appointed April 9th, 1889. He has therefore served as postmaster continuously for nearly twelve years to the perfect satisfaction of his townsmen and the post-office department.

Mr. Brown is a member of the M. E. church, of the G. A. R. and of the American Legion of Honor; he is also a member of the Masonic Fraternity and for two years was master of Richmond Lodge No. 66, F. & A. M.

POSTMASTER GRIFFIN.

OLIVER H. GRIFFIN, whose portrait is herewith presented, fittingly exemplifies the American idea of progression and enterprise, pressing forward with indomitable energy to the accomplishment of greater things, each elevation being the stepping-stone to something more advanced.

He was born in New York city, and came to Staten Island when about six years of age. At fourteen years of age he secured a position as clerk in M. S. Tynan's saw-mill, but soon, having an opportunity for a more lucrative position, he left the saw-mill and took charge of Hall's coal business, which position he held for ten years.

Mr. Griffin then was appointed ticket agent for the S. I. R. T. R. R. Co., at Whitehall street, New York, where his business aptitude quickly won him a high position.

On June 10th, 1890, he received his commission, under the Harrison administration, as postmaster at Stapleton, which office he still fills to the entire satisfaction of the people. It was through his instrumentality that the handsome new post-office building was secured.

Mr. Griffin is active in Masonic matters and the A. O. U. W., is a member of the Staten Island Quartette Club, and for many years has been prominently identified with the Edgewater Fire Department.

SUPT. OF THE POOR BOWEN.

WILLIAM BOWEN was born in Boston in 1840 and was educated in the grammar schools of that city. The family moved to New York when William was fifteen years of age. When he became of age he embarked in the liquor business and, previous to his removal to Staten Island in 1868, was owner of a wholesale liquor store at 31 Broadway. He was proprietor of the New York hotel at Vanderbilt Landing from 1868 to 1889, when he retired from business and removed to his present residence, the Leaycraft homestead, on Simonson avenue.

In 1873, Mr. Bowen was appointed superintendent of the poor of the town of Southfield, for one year, to fill the vacancy caused by the death of Capt. Coppers. At the expiration of his term he was re-elected on the Democratic ticket and has held the office continuously since except one term when the Democratic ticket known as the "3-B" ticket, (Brown for sheriff, Brick for member of assembly and Bowen for superintendent of the poor), was defeated.

Mr. Bowen's term of office is noted in the annals of Richmond county politics for the vigorous fight which he and Mr. Clark made against the "poor-house combine," which resulted in securing an act of the legislature abolishing the office of superintendent of the poor and reviving the office of poor-master, and making the poor-master and the keeper of the alms-house responsible to the board of supervisors.

One of the results of Mr. Bowen's fight against the "poor-house combine" was the capture of the Democratic convention in 1889 by the ring politicians and the defeat of Mr. Bowen for the nomination. He, however, received the unanimous nomination on the Republican ticket and the individual endorsement of the better class of Democrats. At the election he ran over 1,600 ahead of his ticket and was elected by a handsome majority.

A desperate effort was made to count him out by forged election returns, but the work was so bunglingly done that the fraud was discovered and defeated.

COLLECTOR PAUL LATOURETTE.

PAUL LATOURETTE, for many years the tax collector of the town of Northfield, was born at Summerville, S. I., August 11th, 1830, and belongs to the old Latourette family which settled on Staten Island nearly two centuries ago.

In his early life, Mr. Latourette followed the water and was an oyster planter on a large scale.

He was collector for the town of Northfield in 1883 and has held the office continuously since that time, except that he refuses the nomination every third year.

On July 20th, 1851, he was married to Miss Jane Lyons. They have four children:

Paul, Jr., born April 7th, 1852, married June 7th, 1874, to Miss Marietta Wheeler, and lives at Mariners' Harbor. They have six children, May, George, Paul, Sadie, Maude and Florence.

Alonzo, born Dec. 25th, 1853, married Jan. 10th, 1875, to Miss Carrie Smith, and lives at Summerville. They have three children, Gertrude, Louis and Jane.

Christopher C., unmarried, living at Summerville.

Jane, born Jan. 1st, 1860, married May 20th, 1878, to John Wheeler of Staten Island. They live in Brooklyn, and have three children, Charles, Christopher and Paul.

HIGHWAY COMMISSIONER SIMONSON.

CORNELIUS SIMONSON, JR., highway commissioner for the town of Northfield, belongs to the old Simonson family which came from Holland in 1662 and purchased large tracts of land on Staten Island, where they have since lived, useful and respected members of the community.

Cornelius Simonson, Jr., was born in 1840 at the homestead of his branch of the family, in Chelsea, and was educated in the Staten Island schools and has always lived on the farm. Mr. Simonson is a Democrat, and in 1890 he was elected a member of the board of assessors, and in 1893 was elected highway commissioner.

He has always been looked upon as one of the solid sterling men of Northfield, one who honors the office he holds more than the office honors him.

Mr. Simonson married, in 1870, Miss Maria Stellenwerf of Long Island.

JUSTICE ACKER.

AUGUSTUS ACKER was born in the city of New York, November 30th, 1860, of German parentage, was educated in the public schools of that city, and when graduated at the age of seventeen years, he entered the law office of his brother, Edward A. Acker, and began studying for the bar.

In 1877, he came to Staten Island, and made New Brighton his home, where in February 1889, he was elected justice of the peace, and on the following November, justice of the court of sessions, and in 1893, was re-elected justice of the peace and justice of the court of sessions, receiving the largest majority ever given, both of which offices he now holds.

Judge Acker probably hears more important cases than any other justice in the entire county, and his thorough knowledge of the law, and the uniform fairness with which all his judgments are rendered, have given him the title of "the model justice."

While fearless and impartial in the performance of his duty, his strict administration of justice is tempered with that mercy which wells from his sympathetic heart and perennial good nature.

Mr. Acker married Miss Caroline Almstaedt, of New Brighton, on March 26th, 1883, and he has an interesting family of three children, two daughters and one son.

JUSTICE FISHER.

GEO. W. FISHER, eldest son of George Fisher, was born in New York in 1865. In 1866, the family moved to Staten Island and settled in the town of Middletown. In 1884, they purchased the farm near New Springville, where the family have since resided.

In 1892, Mr. Fisher was elected justice of the peace for the town of Northfield, and is probably the youngest justice in Richmond county, but his decisions have been marked by an impartiality and legal knowledge which have won for him the confidence and respect, even of his opponents.

In 1890, Mr. Fisher married Miss Mary Miller of New Springville. They have two children, Walter Irving, aged two years, and Ethel, aged one year.

JUSTICE LANGTON.

DAVID M. LANGTON was born at West New Brighton June 6th, 1854, and has always lived in the same village. He is the youngest son of the late Michael Langton, who was for twenty-four years justice of the peace of the town of Castleton.

Mr. Langton is a mason by trade and in politics is a strong Democrat. He was elected justice of the peace in the spring of 1890 and took office January 1st, 1891. As justice Mr. Langton's rulings have always been upright and fair, and it is his endeavor to make his decisions just and reasonable. His business experience and good judgment have made him a valuable member of the town board.

Mr. Langton married on the 17th of October 1893, Miss Annie Cassidy.

JUSTICE MACORMAC.

SAMUEL A. MACORMAC was born in Stapleton, in 1857, and removed with his family to the town of Westfield, in 1869. He was educated at the Hackettstown Institute at Hackettstown, N. J. After his graduation he took a position as clerk in the store of Seguine & Decker at Rossville, where he remained three years. He was afterward freight clerk on the steamer New Brunswick for five years and on the steamer Saratoga, of the Troy line, for six months. In 1886, he married Carrie M., daughter of the late John A. Ridner, of Greenridge. He purchased the store and business of his late father-in-law, and was appointed postmaster in 1887, which office he holds at the present time. In 1892, he was elected justice of the peace, taking office January 1st, 1893, and associate justice of sessions to take office January 1st, 1894.

Mr. Macormac has always been known as a good, careful business man and is a clear-headed magistrate and a valuable member of the town board.

Mr. and Mrs. Macormac have one son, Frank V., aged three years.

JUSTICE MINNAHAN.

John E. Minnahan, justice of the peace of the town of Castleton, recently appointed to the vacancy caused by the death of Mr. John K. Hall, is at the present time the youngest justice in the Empire state, being in his 25th year. Born in West New Brighton, he has continued to live there up to the present time. After graduating from the local schools he took a course of instruction in the Christian Brothers, school of New York city, graduating with high honors. He is unmarried and resides with his parents. Mr. Minnahan is a member of several societies and holds the honored position of president of the Catholic Union Dramatic Club, being one of its originators, and devotes considerable of his time to amateur theatricals. As a humorist he is often heard in our various amusement halls, especially when the cause is a charitable one, as his services are always gratuitous.

The judge is one of the most companionable young men that you can possibly meet, and he counts his friends by the hundred.

JUSTICE TIERNAN.

PETER TIERNAN, justice of the peace of the town of Middletown, was born in Ireland, but came to America in 1851 and settled in Tompkinsville.

Mr. Tiernan has always taken an active and prominent part in county and local affairs, and as early as 1853 was elected school trustee, which office he held for two terms and the office of school collector for three terms; and in 1876 and 1880 he was tax collector for the town of Middletown. He is now serving his eighth term of justice of the peace, and is the oldest justice in Richmond county. At the expiration of this present term of office he will have served the county thirty-two years in that capacity.

He has also served for fifteen years as a member of Neptune Fire Engine Co. No. 6, and eight years in the 69th Reg't. N. Y. S. M.

Mr. Tiernan has always been a Democrat and taken a prominent part in councils of his party in which he wielded no inconsiderable influence. His court has always maintained a high reputation for the justice and impartiality of his decisions.

JUSTICE CASEY.

WILLIAM C. CASEY, of New Brighton, was born in Ireland in 1848. He came to America while quite young, and after spending some time in San Francisco and Chicago came to Staten Island and settled in New Brighton, in 1867. He has been a justice of the peace of the town of Castleton for the past fifteen years, and served two terms as justice of the sessions; and has been a member of the Democratic County General Committee for nineteen consecutive years. He has also been a member of the school board of school District No. 4 of Castleton for the past nine years and chairman of the board for six years.

Mr. Casey is one of the best known justices on the Island and has heard and decided many important cases with judicial fairness.

PRESIDENT JOHNSTONE.

LOUIS MORRIS JOHNSTONE comes of an old New York family. He was born in New York city in 1839, and passed the early years of his life there. His father, Francis U. Johnstone, M. D., was a prominent physician of that city, who died in 1858. Mr. Johnstone was in South America at the beginning of the Rebellion, but returned to the United States in October 1863, and served as 1st Lieut. of Battery I, Independent Penn., Light Artillery, (commonly known in the Army of the Potomac as Nevin's Battery), from January 12th, 1864, to the close of the war.

In 1879, Mr. Johnstone left New York and came to Staten Island to be near his brother, the late Dr. F. U. Johnstone, of New Brighton. In May 1886, he moved into the third ward, the "Hill district" of the village of Edgewater, and in June of the same year, was elected trustee from that ward, was re-elected in June 1888, '90 and '91, and has held the position of president of the village without opposition since June 1887.

He has been assiduous in the discharge of his official duties, and his retention in office seems to prove that he has won the confidence of his fellow-citizens.

PRESIDENT EGBERT.

GEORGE T. EGBERT was born July 30th, 1851, at Erastina, near the place where he now resides. At twelve years of age he entered the Mt. Washington Collegiate Institute, of New York city.

After passing through the course of study and graduating with high honors, he began business with the firm of Gasherie, Emery & Co., 48 Walker street, New York, one of the largest dry goods jobbers and importers in the city. By strict attention to business he soon rose to the position of book-keeper for that house.

After remaining with the above firm for seven or eight years, Mr Egbert resigned his position, and in 1876 accepted the position of cashier with the Consolidated Fireworks Company of America, 9 and 11 Park place, with a capital of $2,500,000, the largest manufacturers and importers of fire-works and celebration goods in the world; having branches in Chicago, Cincinnati, Rochester, Boston, Baltimore and St. Louis, and doing a business of $1,500,000 annually, their trade covering not only the United States, but extending to Canada, Mexico, South America, Europe and the Sandwich Islands. The principal factories are at Graniteville, and cover sixty acres, but the company has smaller factories at nearly all its branches. It has been awarded the contracts for all the large pyrotechnic displays given in this country in recent years.

At the last annual meeting of the stockholders, Mr. Egbert, who is a large stockholder, was unanimously elected secretary, a position which he now holds.

He is one of the charter members of the Northfield Building Loan Association, one of the most prosperous organizations of the kind in the state, its monthly receipts being $6,500. He has been a member of the board of education for the past five years and was unanimously re-elected at the last school meeting.

Mr. Egbert has been a member of Summerfield Methodist Episcopal Church for nearly twenty years and has filled, at different times, every position of honor and trust in the church, being now president of the board of trustees, and the church has been greatly benefited by his services and liberality.

In politics, Mr. Egbert is a straight out Cleveland Democrat, having voted for him three times for president. He is also active in local politics, in favor of honest government and local improvements.

He was president of the board of sewer commissioners, until he resigned to accept the office of trustee of the village of Port Richmond, to which he was elected at the last charter election. At the first meeting of the new board of trustees, he was elected president.

TRUSTEE KERR.

JAMES KERR, the subject of our sketch, was born in Chatham, near Detroit, Mich., March 20th, 1858, and was educated in Toronto, Canada. He entered the drug business in 1873, and was graduated from the Ontario College of Pharmacy as a pharmaceutical chemist in 1878. When less than twenty years of age he opened a drug store in Toronto, but immature business qualifications precipitated by a general depression in business concluded this venture. A little disfigured by this encounter, but not divested of his monumental pluck and nerve, he turned his footsteps toward the Empire state and the only New York city. After clerking for a time in Brooklyn he finally was induced by Mr. L. Johnson (the originator and proprietor of the now famous Johnson's Happy Pills), to accept a position in his pharmacy at West New Brighton. After satisfying Mr. Johnson of his business tact and energy he was admitted as a partner, and this relation was maintained to the satisfaction of both parties for five years, only ending with Mr. Johnson's retirement from the business, on a comfortable competence. Since Mr. Kerr's residence on Staten Island he has been the recipient of many favors from his fellow townsmen, who know how to appreciate an active, energetic businessman, and all who have been associated with him He has served seven years as an active member of Medora Hook & Ladder Co., No 3, filling all the offices and serving as foreman for three years.

Mr. Kerr is an Odd Fellow, a director in the Staten Island Building Loan and Savings Association, trustee of Richmond Lodge, No. 66, F. & A. M., high priest of Tyrian Chapter, 219, Royal Arch Masons, and last but not least, was chosen at the last charter election to represent the fourth ward of the village of West Brighton, as its alderman.

In conclusion, it would not be out of place to state that we confidently believe that the extraordinary efforts put forward by Mr. Kerr to increase his already large business will be crowned with success.

JOHN J. FETHERSTON.

JOHN J. FETHERSTON has been a life-long resident of Richmond county. Though engaged in private business he has always been prominently identified with public life.

Mr. Fetherston bears a striking resemblance to Senator David B. Hill. He has been a steadfast Democrat all his life and has served with signal success in the Democratic General Committee for the past twenty years. He was chief of the North Shore Fire Department for one term, was trustee of the first ward of the village of New Brighton for ten years and president of the village for five terms, which office he resigned to accept the unanimous appointment as village treasurer, which office he now holds. Though quiet and unassuming, his straightforward course while in office of trust has made him a host of friends among people of all classes.

VILLAGE CLERK O'GRADY.

JOSEPH F. O'GRADY, town clerk of the town of Castleton, and village clerk of the village of New Brighton, was born in the city of New York and has been a resident of Richmond county since he was one year old. He attended St. Peter's Academy at New Brighton, after which he went to Grammar School No. 29, in Greenwich street, New York, from which he was graduated. He then took a two years' course in Latin and Greek in the College of St. Francis Xavier, from there going to Manhattan Academy, where he was graduated in 1880. He immediately accepted a position as teacher in public school No. 4, Tompkinsville, where he remained until 1890. He resigned the vice-principalship of the school to accept the office of village clerk. He has been unanimously re-appointed four times.

Mr. O'Grady has an extensive acquaintanceship and hopes some day to become prominently identified with the Democracy of Richmond county.

VILLAGE CLERK COLLINS.

MICHAEL J. COLLINS was born in Brooklyn, in 1856. When he was six years of age, his family moved to Staten Island, where Michael, after a course of study in the public schools, studied the classics under a private tutor.

After completing his education, he returned to Brooklyn, where he remained in business for four years, after which he returned to Staten Island. In 1884, he was appointed secretary to the board of health, and in 1886 was made clerk of the village of Edgewater, and the fact that he has held this position for seven consecutive years, under different boards of trustees, is the best proof of how well he has performed the duties of his office.

Mr. Collins has also served as a member of the board of directors of the Edgewater Co-operative Building and Loan Association, is a member of the Southfield Lodge, Ancient Order of United Workmen 401, has been treasurer of the Forester's Court, Staten Island, for the past six years, and is one of the charter members of the Edgewater C. B. L.

Mr. Collins is a Democrat, always active in politics, and has served as secretary of several conventions.

BUSINESS AND PROFFESSIONAL MEN.

FRANK S. GANNON.

FRANK S. GANNON, general superintendent of the Staten Island Rapid Transit railroad, and the New York division of the Baltimore and Ohio railroad, was born September 16th, 1851, at Spring Valley, Rockland county, New York. He entered railway service in 1868, as telegraph operator on the Delaware division of the Erie railroad. In April 1870, he was appointed clerk in the office of the president of the Jersey Midland railroad, now known as the New York, Susquehanna and Western railroad, and served consecutively as president's clerk and train despatcher. In April 1875, he was made train despatcher of the Long Island railway, was promoted to be depot master in 1876 and master of transportation in 1877, which position he held until January 1881, when he was made supervisor of trains on the Pittsburg division of the Baltimore and Ohio railroad. He had held this position but three months when he was appointed general superintendent of the New York and Northern railroad. In August 1886, he resigned his position to take the office of general superintendent of the Staten Island Rapid Transit railroad, which position he now holds, together with that of general superintendent of the New York division of the Baltimore and Ohio railroad, to which he was appointed in March 1890.

Mr. Gannon is also a director of the Staten Island Rapid Transit Railroad Company, a director of the John Good Cordage and Machine Company, president of the Richmond Land Company, president of the Rapid Transit branch of the Co-operative Building Bank of New York, treasurer of the employes' Mutual Benefit Association, member of the Manhattan Club of New York, and chairman of the executive committee of the New York and New Jersey Car Service Association.

Mr. Gannon is a thorough railroad man, a strict disciplinarian, and progressive.

FRANK S. GANNON,
Superintendent S. I. R. T. R. R. Co.

Many improvements have been made in the rules' and methods of operating the road since he has been at the helm. Trains have been multiplied, the time shortened, new cars and engines provided, new and handsome stations built, large and commodious ferryboats built, a new ferry-house in New York, and the foundations laid for a handsome new ferry-house at St. George. The track has been doubled to New Dorp, and arrangements are being made to complete the double track to Tottenville and build several more new stations.

Mr. Gannon has also abolished the old system of giving passes to favored patrons and compelling all others to pay transient fares and has adopted a system of commutation, half fare and family tickets which has proved a great advantage to permanent residents of the Island.

Personally, Mr. Gannon is one of the most genial of men and has the confidence and esteem alike of the public and the large force of employes under his control.

B. KREISCHER & SONS.

The business of B. Kreischer & Sons was established at Kreischerville in 1852, by Balthasar Kreischer. Mr. Kreischer was born in Germany in 1813, where he learned the business of stone-cutter and sculptor. He came to America soon after the fire of 1835, which destroyed a great portion of New York city. For a while he carried on the trade of master builder, and erected many buildings in the burned district. Soon afterward, having discovered large deposits of fire clay in New Jersey, he began the manufacture of fire-brick at 58 Goerck street, New York; his business increased rapidly, and in about the year 1852 he discovered the extensive clay deposits in the vicinity of the present village of Kreischerville.

With a keen foresight, he bought up large quantities of land including nearly all of the best clay banks in the vicinity, and set to work to build one of the largest fire-brick factories to be found in this country, where the industry was then in its infancy.

Mr. Kreischer then gathered around him men skilled in the manufacture of fire-brick, and was able from the first to turn out an article superior to the best imported bricks. The works have been twice completely destroyed by fire, once in 1867 and again in 1892, and each time they have been rebuilt, more complete than before.

PROMINENT MEN OF STATEN ISLAND, 1893.

THE LATE B. KREISCHER.

In all its machinery and methods, the factory has kept pace with the latest improvements of the times, and its brand of goods has always commanded the highest prices; and while other factories have closed up or curtailed their production, this factory has always pressed forward with a steady growth of capacity and output.

The large and thriving village which has grown up and around this single industry shows how important a part it has paid in the prosperity of this end of Staten Island. One important branch of this industry, aside from fire-brick, is the manufacture of gas retorts, an invention especially due Mr. Kreischer. These retorts are in use in nearly every city in the Union.

Mr. Kreischer was also one of the originators of the Staten Island Railroad Company, and was for a time president, and during his term, he instituted many improvements, which were of lasting benefit to the road.

When the Staten Island factory was built the manufacture of fire-brick in New York was abandoned, but the New York office was retained, at which nearly all of the business was transacted. In 1871, George F. Kreischer, the eldest son, was taken into partnership by his father, and he assumed charge of the New York office.

In 1878, Charles C. and Edward B., the two younger sons, were taken into the co-partnership, and the firm assumed the style and title of B. Kreischer & Sons, as it exists to-day.

Mr. Kreischer was a type of man too rarely seen in this country, where there is little sympathy or mutual interest between employer and employe.

He always took a lively interest in all that pertained to the personal welfare of his employes, and considered it both a duty and a pleasure to advise and help them, and two of the latest acts of his life were to build a handsome church and school-house and to establish a mutual benefit society for the relief of the sick and injured. Both Mr. Kreischer and his sons contributed liberally to the funds of this society and took a personal interest in its success, and thus enabled their men to be self-supporting in time of sickness, instead of being obliged to depend on charity. In a thousand ways Mr. Kreischer showed an interest in the welfare of his employes that went beyond the question of mere work and wages, and seldom has an employer been more sincerely mourned by all classes than Mr. Kreischer, whose death occurred in 1886 at his home in Kreischerville.

CHARLES C. KREISCHER.

CHARLES C., the second son of the late Balthasar Kreischer, was born in New York city, Sept. 15th, 1850. He received his first schooling in the German schools of the city, after which he took a course of study in St. Francis Zavier's College, which was supplemented by a thorough commercial education at Bryant & Stratton's Business College.

After completing his education, his father placed him in his large fire-brick factory at Kreischerville, where he learned, practically, every branch of the work in order to fit him thoroughly for the responsible position which he was afterward to take, as general overseer of the manufacturing branch of his father's business.

After spending two years in the factory, Mr. Kreischer went to Germany and entered the Polytechnic University at Zurich, Switzerland, where he remained four years. On his return he again went into the factory at Kreischerville, and in 1872 was made superintendent of the factory. In 1878, he was made a member of the firm of B. Kreischer & Sons, and at the opening of the New York Anderson Pressed Brick factory, he was made superintendent of that business, which he managed successfully until the spring of 1891, when he resigned and went to Europe.

Mr. Kreischer has held several town offices and has been trustee of the Kreischerville school district for the last twenty years and an elder in St. Peter's Church since it was organized. He is the first regent of Arthur Kill Council 1408, Royal Arcanum, and a member of Huguenot Lodge 381, F. & A. M., and Staten Island Chapter 145, R. A. M.

On June 19th, 1879, Mr. Kreischer married Antonia G., second daughter of Mr. George Wanier, of New York. Mr. and Mrs. Kreischer have one son, Arthur G., aged eleven years, now a student at St. Austin's school, New Brighton.

Mr. Kreischer has always been a staunch Democrat and has wielded a potent influence in the councils of the party, and has often been tendered the nomination for important offices, but has preferred to devote his time to his large business interests.

EDWARD B., the youngest of the children of the late Balthasar Kreischer, was born in New York city February 18th, 1853. He was educated in the public schools in the city and was graduated with honor from Packard's Business College. His first experience in business was as book-keeper in his father's office in New York. He remained there but a short time, when he was appointed purchasing agent and paying teller for Steinway & Sons' great piano house.

When his father was appointed president of the Staten Island railway, Mr. Kreischer was put in charge of the ticket department and had the management of all the stations along the line of the road.

In 1877, Mr. Kreischer entered the factory at Kreischerville, and in 1878, was made a member of the firm of B. Kreischer & Sons, and from that time to the present has been, either in connection with his brother Charles C., or alone, the manager of the manufacturing department of the business.

In 1884, Mr. Kreischer built the handsome residence on the hill above the factory, where he now resides. He has held the office for school collector at Kreischerville for the past fourteen years, he has been an elder in St. Peter's German Evangelical Lutheran Church since it was established, is treasurer of the church, of the Mutual Aid Society of the employes of B. Kreischer & Sons and is vice-regent of Arthur Kill Council 1408, Royal Arcanum. On June 19th, 1877, Mr. Kreischer married Freda, eldest daughter of Mr. George Wanier, then of New York city, but now living at Kreischerville. They have one son, Harry A., aged fourteen years, a student of St. Austin's school at New Brighton.

Mr. Kreischer is a thorough business man and manages with marked ability and success the large business established by his father and still conducted under the name of B. Kreischer & Sons.

HON. E. P. DOYLE.

Hon. Edward P. Doyle was born at Mariners' Harbor, June 8th, 1860. He was graduated from the public schools at the age of twelve years, and took his first position in a New York ship broker's office, after which he spent eleven years with a wholesale shoe house.

He was secretary of the Democratic congressional convention for this district in 1882, and was chairman of the county convention in 1883. He was elected member of assembly in 1885, and gained the reputation of being one of the hardest workers in that body.

It was largely owing to his indefatigable labor that the present oyster law and many laws for the protection of fish and oysters were placed on the statute books of this state.

Mr. Doyle was supervisor for the town of Northfield from 1886 to 1891, and was one of the hardest working and most efficient members of the board. From 1886 to 1892, he was secretary of the joint commission for fixing the boundary between the states of New York and New Jersey. He is and has been since 1887, secretary and engineer of the New York Fish Commission, was secretary of the old New York Free Trade Club, was the first secretary of the Reform Club, and American correspondent of the Cobden Club, is a member of the Reform and Commonwealth Clubs and of the Staten Island Cricket Club, is president and treasurer of the Staten Island Produce Company, secretary and treasurer of the Aquahonga and the Manor Park Land Companies, secretary of the Northfield and Prohibition Park Building and Loan Associations, secretary of the finance committee of Co-operative Building Bank, a trustee of the Richmond County Savings Bank, and a member of the firm of Reedy & Co.

It will be seen that Mr. Doyle is a very busy man, working both with his head and hands, and that he has played no small part in the material advancement of Staten Island.

JOHN H. ELSWORTH.

JOHN H. ELSWORTH son of Capt. Wm. Elsworth, was born at Bayonne, N. J., in 1843. He was educated in the schools at Bayonne, and remained there in business with his brothers, who were extensive oyster planters, until 1877, when he came to Staten Island and entered into co-partnership with his present partner, Capt. Peter Polworth, in the oyster planting business, in which line the firm has always done a successful business and attained a high financial rating.

Mr. Elsworth has always been a staunch, hardworking and active Republican. In 1888, he received the unanimous nomination of the Richmond County Republican Convention, for the office of sheriff, and was elected by nearly two hundred majority, although it was a presidential year and Cleveland carried the county by nearly nineteen hundred. A desperate effort was made to defeat his election on forged returns, but the fraud was discovered in time to prevent his defeat, and he was triumphantly ushered into office, Jan. 1st, 1889.

During his term of office Sheriff Elsworth was often publicly complimented by the supreme court judges, and by the county judge, on the efficient and faithful manner in which he performed the duties of the office, and at the close of his official term Justice Cullen, of the supreme court, and the members of the county bar, irrespective of party, paid a high tribute to the manner in which Mr. Elsworth had performed his duties during his entire term.

Mr. Elsworth comes of a sea-faring family, noted for their skill in seamanship, his father having been a captain of a coasting vessel, at the early age of fourteen years. His brother Philip was a successful designer of yachts. Among the famous craft designed by him were the Montague, the Grayling and the Atlantic. His brother Joseph was one of the most skillful skippers that ever sailed in New York harbor. He commanded the Puritan in its race against the English yacht Genesta, and the May Flower against the Galatea, in both of which races he was successful, and won the cup.

Mr. Elsworth was married on the thirty-fourth anniversary of his birthday, June 21st, 1877, to Miss Elizabeth W. Jones, daughter of James S. Jones, of Snow Hill, Md. They have no children.

JOHN L. DAILEY.

JOHN LINDERMAN DAILEY.

JOHN LINDERMAN DAILEY, the only son of the Rev. J. P. Dailey, was born in 1853, at Flemington, N. J., where his father was stationed as the pastor of the Methodist Episcopal church. His mother was a direct descendant of Gen. Daniel Brodhead, one of Washington's most able and trusted officers during the Revolution.

In 1874, Mr. Dailey's father was appointed pastor of St. Paul's Church, Tottenville, and the family came to Staten Island to live, and since that time Mr. Dailey has been a resident of Tottenville.

He was always a staunch Republican and early took to politics, his first campaign being for the office of justice of the peace in 1877 for which he received the nomination of both parties. In 1883, and again in 1886, he was elected highway commissioner, being the only man on the ticket elected in 1886. In 1885, he ran for member of assembly against the late Edward A. Moore, and again in 1889 against Daniel T. Cornell, when he had the highest vote of any man on the ticket and was beaten by only about 300 majority, while the average Democratic majority was over 1,100.

In January 1889, on the accession of John H. Elsworth to the office of sheriff, Mr. Dailey was appointed under-sheriff and remained in office till the close of Mr. Elsworth's term.

During his term of office as under-sheriff, Judge Cullen publicly complimented Mr. Dailey from the bench upon the prompt and efficient manner in which he performed the duties of his office, and at the last term of the county court, before Sheriff Elsworth's term of office expired Judge Stephens spoke in the highest terms of the manner in which the sheriff and under-sheriff had conducted the office through their entire term, and the members of the bar of Richmond county unanimously passed resolutions to the same effect.

In 1891, Mr. Dailey received the unanimous nomination of the Republican convention to the office of sheriff and came within 115 votes of election, although Roswell P. Flower, for governor, carried the county by nearly 1,600 majority.

There is no Republican in Richmond county who can point to a record of political campaigns which have so reduced the large majorities usually polled by the Democratic party as Mr. John L. Dailey, and he has often been called the "most popular man in Richmond county."

WILLIAM S. BACOT.
Ex-County Road Engineer.

WILLIAM SINCLAIR BACOT, member of the American Society of Civil Engineers, was born at East Orange, N. J., April 19th, in the year 1860.

His family is descended from the French Huguenots, of Touraine, France, who settled in the colony of South Carolina, at Charleston, in the year 1694.

His father, Robert C. Bacot, came north in 1838 and married Mary Gilchrist, likewise of French descent, the granddaughter of John Vacher, a surgeon who served with the Continental army in the Revolution. He took up his residence in New York and subsequently in New Jersey, where he and his family have lived ever since. Robert C. Bacot, following his profession, now holds the position of chief engineer of the Riparian Commission of the state of New Jersey, to which he was appointed in 1865.

William Sinclair Bacot was schooled in Hudson county, New Jersey, and entered Princeton College in the year 1877.

After pursuing a course of engineering in that institution he was graduated in the year 1881. Several years later he received from that college the degree of Civil Engineer.

For the first five years after his college career Mr. Bacot devoted his time to the study of engineering, practicing meanwhile in the capacity of assistant on several important public works. He first filled the place of second assistant on the construction of the Hackensack water-works under Charles B. Brush, C. E., now vice-president of the American Society of Civil Engineers, and afterward as first assistant on the water-works of Greenwich, Conn., Mount Vernon, and Fishkill, N. Y. In the course of events he became chief engineer of the last three mentioned works, which position he still holds on those at Greenwich. While so acting many other engineering projects have fallen to his task, prominent among which may be noticed the preliminary planning of the new water supply for the city of Albany, and the construction of a system of Telford roads in the village of Lenox, Mass.

Shortly after the passage of the county roads act in June 1890, he was appointed to the position of county engineer, by the board of supervisors, of Richmond county. The results of his efforts are too well-known to need further description.

Mr. Bacot is a Mason, a member of Tompkins Lodge No. 471, F. & A. M., and is also enrolled in the membership of many other organizations on the Island and lsewhere.

BENJAMIN BROWN.

BENJAMIN BROWN came to Staten Island in 1853 from New York, where he was reared and educated. His first entrance into politics was in 1861, when he was elected to the office of constable on the Democratic ticket. In 1869, after one of the hardest fights known in local politics, he was elected trustee of the village of Edgewater, which office he held for several years, serving also one term as president of the board.

In 1876, he was elected to the office of sheriff, and at the expiration of his term was elected treasurer and collector for the village of Edgewater which offices he held for three years when, in 1882, he was again elected sheriff. At the expiration of his second term, he was made under-sheriff under John J. Vaughan, Jr., thus serving nine years as sheriff and under-sheriff.

During the days of the old Volunteer Fire Department, Mr. Brown was the prime mover in organizing the Edgewater Fire Department and was for a time its president and treasurer, and for six years its chief engineer. Soon after the breaking out of the Civil war, he helped to organize the fifth Ira Harris Cavalry, and was its first forage master.

He is a strong advocate of Loan Associations and always endeavors to impress upon the working man the benefits to be derived by joining them and owning his home.

In 1887, he organized Pioneer Lodge of the Ancient Order of United Workmen which lodge soon reached a membership of two hundred; this organization is a benevolent order or life insurance and has paid for its sick and deceased brethren over seventy thousand dollars in this short space of time. He was made district deputy the same year and has organized ten lodges in this county. The tenth lodge Vigilant, No. 429, was instituted on November 11th with the largest list of charter members of any that has yet been organized in the county.

Mr. Brown is now engaged in the coal and wood business at Stapleton, having purchased the long established coal yard of S. C. Hall, where he is doing a thriving and prosperous business.

JOHN S. WARDE,
Superintendent S. I. Water Supply Co.

John S. Warde, only son of Mary J. and the late William D. Warde, was born near Tarrytown, Westchester county, in 1840. He was educated at Tarrytown, and when only thirteen years of age, he was appointed by Isaac V. Fowler, then postmaster of New York city, to a position in the New York post-office, where he remained until the war broke out in 1861, when he resigned his position and became a member of Company I, of the 9th Regiment N. Y. S. Militia, afterward known as the 83rd N. Y. State Volunteers.

Mr. Warde took quite an active part in raising and equiping the above company, and they left New York June 17th, 1861, to join the regiment which was then at the front, in General Patterson's division, Army of the Potomac. In 1864, he was transferred to the 104th, N. Y. S. Volunteers, and after the surrender of Lee, was mustered out of the service under general order. No. 25.

Upon his return to New York, Mr. Warde was appointed to a position in the Erie R. R. under O. H. P. Archer. Some time after this, the Mercantile Safe Deposit Co. was organized, one of the first companies of the kind in New York, and having been tendered a position with them, he severed his connection with the Erie.

In 1873, Mr. Warde moved to Brooklyn, and a short time afterward, obtained a position in the water department of the City Works Department. He was assigned to the purveyors' department under Peter Millne. In 1881, he resigned and came to Staten Island as superintendent of the S. I. Water Supply Company.

When Mr. Warde assumed charge the company possessed one engine, one boiler and fifteen miles of pipe, with a capacity of 1,000,000 gallons per day. There are now three engines, three boilers, about fifty miles of pipe, and the daily capacity is over 5,000,000.

In 1885, he became a member of Medora H. & L. Co., No. 3, and has represented that company in the board of representatives of the North Shore Fire Department since that time. He was vice-president of the board for two years, and he is now serving his sixth term as president. He was on the committee chosen to draw up the articles of incorporation, and was a leading member of the committee instrumental in having the department incorporated. He is also a member of Scotia Lodge F. & A. M., of New York city, and of Tyrian Chapter R. A. M., of Staten Island, of Richmond Post G. A. R., also Staten Island Council, Royal Arcanum, and Staten Island Lodge, Knights of Pythias, of which he is past chancellor commander.

In politics, Mr. Warde has always been an active Republican, and has been on the General Committee from Castleton nearly all the years of his residence on Staten Island. In 1892, he was the Republican candidate for supervisor from the town of Castleton, and although defeated by Robert Moore, Democrat, he reduced his Democratic opponent's usually large majority of from 500 to 800, to 268.

In 1861, two months previous to his enlistment, Mr. Warde married Miss Lizzie Jean Clark, daughter of Mary E. and the late George W. Clark, a well-known New York artist. Mr. and Mrs. Warde have two sons, Charles S. and John S. Jr., the former of whom was married in 1892 to Miss Luqueer Meylert, of Port Richmond, and has one child, Charles S., Jr

HORACE E. BUEL.

HORACE E. BUEL, chairman of the Republican General Committee, is the eldest son of Orlando W. Buel. He was born on Staten Island, October 1852. His father settled on the Island in 1836 and established the marble cutting business at Port Richmond, where the business is still carried on by Mr. Buel and his father. In 1871, he joined Fire Engine Company No. 3, of the Port Richmond Fire Department, in which he has held every office up to that of chief. He is also a member of the board of health of the village of Port Richmond.

Mr. Buel has always been connected with, and is a prominent working member of the Republican party, but has never been an aspirant for political favors or lucrative offices. He has been a member of the General Committee about ten years, and at the organization of the last General Committee, he was elected chairman without opposition.

Mr. Buel is a man of quiet and unassuming manners, but with a clear head and a good stock of hard common sense, and is just the man to keep a political organization harmonious and united and to keep it in good fighting order.

CALVIN DETRICK.

CALVIN DETRICK, second son of Samuel and Catharine Detrick, was born at Stroudsburg, Pa. His father was a farmer, and farm air, food and associations strengthened in young Detrick the qualities of mind and of body that afterward proved invaluable to him.

The scholastic year at the nearest school never exceeded three months. This was not to the liking of either the father or son, so the latter, when he was about sixteen, was sent to the Stroudsburg Academy, at which he applied himself closely to his books for three years.

Shortly before he attained his twentieth year he went into business with a friend, the firm bearing the name of Pinchot & Detrick. They had a country store at Milford, Pa., and did a thriving business. Mr. Detrick longed, however, for the greater opportunities afforded by a city. He, therefore, sought and obtained employment in a wholesale drygoods and notions house in New York. He posted himself thoroughly in this business which was not quite to his fancy, so with a ready adaptability we next find him a contractor in Philadelphia, where he engaged in the laying of sewers, erection of water-works, the building of stone foundations and similar work.

He came to Staten Island in the spring of 1884 and introduced the present system of supplying water into the village of Edgewater.

In the Spring of 1858 he created and organized the Richmond Light, Heat and Power Co. which now furnishes New Brighton with electric lighting. He was its treasurer for some time. Two years later he formed the Staten Island Light, Heat and Power Company, which now furnishes Port Richmond and a part of West Brighton with electric lighting.

Mr. Detrick is in no sense an exploiter. When he forms a company it is formed to stay and he stays with it, putting in his own money freely and then giving his close attention to the details of the enterprise.

Mr. Detrick resides in New Brighton, where he intends to remain. He has invested no small part of his fortune in Staten Island property.

He descended in a direct line from the sturdy Hollanders.

In 1882, Mr. Detrick married Miss Jennie Murray, of Philadelphia. They have three children.

WILLIAM W. CORBETT.

WILLIAM W. CORBETT was born in Birmingham, England, in 1822, and came to America in 1840. In 1843, he went to Canada, where he remained five years. He was married, during his residence in Canada, to Miss Mary Davis. On his return, he worked in New York, until 1851, when he moved to Stapleton to take charge of the sash and blind factory of the late Elwood Taylor. He remained there three years, when he went to Port Richmond, and established a sash and blind factory of his own and carried on a successful business until 1866, when he removed his factory and residence to New Brighton, and continued the business until 1870.

In 1861, under President Lincoln's administration, he was appointed night inspector of customs, of the old Quarantine district at Tompkinsville, and held the position for five years, at the end of which term he was promoted to day inspector with two assistants, and his district included all Staten Island and Bayonne. He remained in this position until the second year of Cleveland's administration.

In 1868, he was elected justice of the peace, which office he held for six consecutive terms. He was justice of the sessions for ten years, and sat on the bench with Judges Metcalfe, Westervelt and Stephens.

In politics, he has always been an active Republican, and was one of the five who organized the Republican party on the North Shore, during the Fremont campaign, and helped to hang the first Republican banner in the county. He was secretary of the first Republican General Committee of the county, of which Geo. William Curtis was president; and has himself served two terms as president of the General Committee.

Mr. Corbett still carries on the real estate business in New Brighton, has been for ten years general manager for the Henderson estate, is agent for the Society for the Prevention of Cruelty to Children, and has been since its organization, and is the head of the Local Detective Agency, recently established on Staten Island, with the approval and co-operation of the county courts and police department.

CAPT. MICHAEL CONKLIN.

CAPT. MICHAEL CONKLIN was born in New York, Sept. 29th, 1828, and was brought up and educated in the city. At the early age of nine years he ran away from home and went to sea. He made several voyages, after which he learned the trade of ship-carpenter, in the shipyard of his father, who was a partner of the late Samuel Secor.

After thoroughly learning his trade he established a shipyard at New Rochelle, where he overhauled and repaired nearly all the racing yachts of that time.

In 1854, he came to Staten Island intending to establish a shipyard near Quarantine, but subsequently changed his plans, and formed a partnership with John E. Armstrong in the business of owning and running boats, instead of building them.

The first vessel they built was the propellor Rescue, the first propellor ever built for towing service outside the harbor. She was employed by the quarantine commissioners during the quarantine season and at the breaking out of the war of the rebellion was chartered by the metropolitan police harbor for patrol. The Rescue and the Washington Hunt were chartered by the government and remained South all through the war.

In 1861, they built the Harriet A. Weed, named after the daughter of the late Thurlow Weed, who was a close personal friend of Capt. Conklin. She was afterward sold to the government and was blown up by the rebels at Newburn. The Harriet A. Weed was also used as a gun boat, and Moses Lyons now living at Tottenville was captain. In 1862, they built the John A. Dix and sold her to the government. This boat is still in the service as light-house tender in southern waters.

In 1863, they bought the Sylvan Shore and put her on the New Brunswick route in opposition to the George Law, but afterward chartered her to the government, and this is the vessel which carried the troops that captured Wilkes Booth after the assassination of President Lincoln. On this trip she ran afoul of a wreck which had been sunk by the rebels and stove a hole in her side. She was kept afloat by putting mattresses in the hole and keeping the steam pumps at work until the boat arrived at Baltimore where she was put on the dry dock.

In 1866, the firm bought the Chicopee and put her on the route from New York to Amboy in opposition to the S. I. Railway and ran her successfully till 1869, when she was purchased by Sharp, Freze & Co. of Bridgetown, N. J., and was run between that place and Philadelphia.

Among the other boats owned and sold by Conklin & Armstrong were the Washington Hunt, the Maryland and the Katalidin.

In 1870, Mr. Conklin joined Wm. Mulford in the lumber and building material business, in Stapleton, and afterward the firm bought the Jessup Mill at Greenridge.

In 1880, Mr. Conklin sold out his interest in the business, and in 1882, when the office of inspector of foreign vessels was created, Mr. Conklin was appointed the first incumbent and held the position until Sept. 15th, 1885, when he was removed by the Democratic administration. In 1889, he was appointed, without solicitation, assistant inspector of mills, and performed the duties of inspector of foreign vessels until 1893, when he was again removed, during Mr. Cleveland's second term.

Mr. Conklin was one of the founders of the Republican party on the south side of the Island, and has always been an active and influential worker in the party. He was for many years intimately associated, politically, with Wm. H. Seward, Thurlow Weed, E. D. Morgan, Moses Taylor and Gen. John A. Dix, and now has in his house at Annadale the desk on which Gen. Dix wrote the famous order, "If any man hauls down the American flag, shoot him on the spot."

DR. REINER ROEHRE.

Dr. R. Roehre, superintendent of the International Ultramarine Works, near Rossville, was born in Bonn, Germany, in 1851, was educated in Bonn, Leipsic and Freibourg, and from the University of Freibourg he took the degree of Doctor of Philosophy in 1879. In 1884, he came to America and took charge of the construction and operation of the International Ultramarine Works which are the largest of the kind in America. Before coming to America Dr. Roehre made himself acquainted with the manufacture of ultramarine and the machinery required for a large plant and was able to construct the works with all the latest improvements for the manufacture and handling of its large output.

The extensive buildings are a net-work of railroads on which all the material is handled by cars at the lowest possible cost of production. Much of the success of the business is due the skill and experience of the doctor, and the output of this factory exceeds that of all other ultramarine factories in the United States combined.

The doctor was married in 1882 to Miss Annie Dittrich of Saxony. They have five children, one boy Rudolph, and four girls, Katharine, Gertrude, Emma and Charlotte.

FRANK RINSCHLER.

FRANK RINSCHLER was born in Balen, Germany, in 1843, Oct. 7th, and learned his trade of mason and builder, in the city of his birth. In 1866, he came to Staten Island and established himself in Tompkinsville and worked in the Light House Department until 1870. In 1878, he established business for himself, locating in Stapleton, where he has since carried on a business, being reckoned one of the foremost builders in the county, taking contracts not only on the Island but in New York, Brooklyn and New Jersey and a large amount of village and county work beside private buildings.

Among the large contracts which Mr. Rinschler has taken, was that for the International Ultramarine Works at Rossville, the largest of the kind in America; the Baltimore flats at Tompkinsville, one of the largest private buildings on the Island; the main building of the new Emigration Bureau on Ellis Island; the Clifton public school built in conjunction with John G. Vaughn, and at the present writing he is erecting the new building for the Drew Theological Seminary at Madison, N. J., costing $125,000.

Mr. Rinschler is one of the crack shots of the Staten Island Schutzen Co., and was captain for the company for two years; has been a member of the Klopstock Lodge F. & A. M. from the first year of its organization, and is a popular and prominent member of a large number of local lodges and societies

PETER ANDROVETTE.

CAPT. PETER ANDROVETTE, the second son of the late Peter Androvette, was born at what is now Kreischerville, in 1834. In 1859, he was married to Anna M., daughter of the late Thomas Marshall, of Woodbridge, N. J. He has two sons, Murray and Alfred, and three daughters, Susie, wife of Alfred Killmeyer, of Kreischerville, Clara, wife of Wm. Toland, of Tottenville, and Lizzie, wife of Henry Scott, of Kreischerville.

Mr. Androvette has always followed the water, having in early life joined the firm of Kreischer & Maurer in the transportation business, and on the dissolution of the firm, he took the general management of the large freighting business of B. Kreischer & Sons.

Among the vessels of which he was master and part owner were the Caroline Kreischer, 90 tons; Magic, 85 tons; Wm. P. Boggs, 70 tons; Mary Robb, 50 tons; John I. Maurer, 75 tons; Mary Heitman, 90 tons.

In 1872, Mr. Androvette saw that steam was coming to the front as the power for rapid transportation and he set to work to build a fleet of steam tugs and lighters. In 1873, he built the steam lighter Clara, 100 tons; in 1878, the steam lighter Flora, 150 tons; in 1882, the steam lighter Harry, 100 tons; and in 1887, he purchased the steam lighter Lizzie M. Conklin, 150 tons, beside the steam tugs Allie and Evie, the Sadie Ellis, Little Nellie and Mabel, and a large number of barges of from 200 to 250 tons capacity.

In 1891, he formed the company known as the Androvette Towing and Transportation Company, incorporated under the laws of the state of New Jersey, of which he has been the president from the time of its organization, capital stock $20,000. The fleet of tugs consists of Allie and Evie, the Mabel and the Geo. B. Roe.

Among the other large enterprises in which Mr. Androvette has been interested was the organization of the Perth Amboy Dry Dock Company, of which he was for a time president.

By shrewd management, untiring industry and strict attention to business, Mr. Androvette has accumulated a comfortable fortune.

He has been a prominent member of Bethel Church for over thirty years, and has been almost constantly in the official board, and since the death of the late Hon. Ephraim J. Totten, has been president of the board of trustees.

JOHN TURNER.

JOHN TURNER was born in County Donegal, Ireland, in 1813, of Scotch Presbyterian parentage. He was brought up and educated in his native place, but, instead of joining the church of his fathers, he became, at an early age, an active member of the Baptist denomination.

In 1832, he came to America and settled in Yorkville, where he engaged in the house-painting business, a trade which he had learned in his native country. During his thirty years' residence in Yorkville, he carried on a large and successful business and was active in church and charitable enterprises. He was largely instrumental in the building of the Park Baptist Church, the first Baptist church in America which had a spire. He also started and furnished the Yorkville reading-room and library, which was afterward burned, but most of the books was saved.

During the draft riots of 1863, Mr. Turner's store, corner of 86th street and 3rd avenue, was burned by the rioters on account of Mr. Turner's well-known union sentiments. Having then accumulated a comfortable fortune, Mr. Turner retired from business and purchased the Lenhart property on Amboy road, near Bethel Church, Tottenville.

In 1873, Mr. Turner exchanged the Lenhart property for his present residence in Brooklyn, and the following year purchased a summer residence on Washington street. He took an active interest in the matter of incorporating the village in 1869, but, becoming dissatisfied with the management of the village affairs, he was as active in getting the charter repealed two years later, in Albany.

Mr. Turner has been, financially, the chief support of the South Baptist Church of Tottenville. He gave the church the site on which it stands and moved it from Johnson avenue to its present location, and built the lecture-room. He has recently given the church the two stores adjoining it, together with a cottage on Arents avenue, and has recently contributed five hundred dollars for further repairs.

Mr. Turner was twice married. By his first wife, who was a native of Edinburgh, Scotland, he had two sons, beside other children. The eldest, John, enlisted in the 10th New York Volunteers, and was killed in the battle of the Wilderness. The other son, Thomas, lives in Brooklyn and holds a position in the Brooklyn post-office. His second wife, who is still living, is of English descent. Before her marriage she had been for over twenty years employed in the book department of the Methodist Book Concern in New York, and since her marriage has been esteemed by all who know her for her many domestic virtues.

Mr. Turner has passed his time for the last few years, during the summer, at Tottenville, at his favorite pastime of fishing, at which he is quite an adept, but for the past year failing health has prevented his indulging in this recreation.

CHARLES WYETH.

CHARLES WYETH was born on the anniversary of the discovery of America, Oct. 12th, 1858, at his present residence, Richmond Hill. He is the son of the accomplished lawyer, Nathaniel J. Wyeth, and was educated in the midst of the masterpieces of knowledge. He was attracted by the "Circle of the Sciences" and chose civil engineering as a profession, and has pursued the development of the applied physical sciences.

Mr. Wyeth was prominent in the location and construction of the Staten Island and North and South Shore railroads, the Crystal Water-works, the Erie and Wyoming Valley railroad from Hawley to Pittston, the Susquehanna and Alleghany railroad, and he was assistant engineer on the Arthur Kill bridge and the S. I. R. T. railroad.

Appreciating the immense resources of the waters of the land and the seas, Mr. Wyeth accepted the appointment of assistant engineer of the commissioners of fisheries of the state of New York, in their extensive hydrographic work. He believes what is worth doing is worth doing well. He is a member of the Engineers' club of Philadelphia.

CALVIN D. VAN NAME.

The subject of this sketch is Calvin Decker Van-Name of Erastina. He was born in the same town, Northfield, on this Island, January 3rd, 1857. His father was William Henry Van Name, a successful oyster planter, who died in Northfield some years ago. The son received the degree of L. L. B. from the University of the City of New York before arriving of age, and was admitted to practice law immediately on reaching twenty-one. Mr. Van Name, although a young man, has long been prominent on Staten Island.

As an attorney he was successful from the beginning. He was entrusted with important matters and acquired a large practice almost as soon as he was admitted to the bar.

He had a long training in the practice of law with L. Bradford Prince, since chief justice and later governor of New Mexico, but then senator from this district. This gave him a complete knowledge of the departments at Albany. That he made a favorable impression there is evidenced by the fact that he has obtained more grants of land under water than any lawyer in the state.

His successful conduct of the Foley South Beach case and the eviction of the Burkes and Lancaster Syms claimants from the Garretsons beach made all holders of old farm titles his lasting friends, and demonstrated the security of Staten Island titles.

His real estate practice is very large, and he has in his safes complete abstracts of the titles to the farms as they once existed in continuous line in Northfield from Bodine's Mill to Howland's Hook.

The Van Name family is the largest on Staten Island, and Mr. Van Name is related to all the branches. All are descendants of the old Hollander Jochem Engelbert VanNamen, who came here from Heusden in the ship Hope which sailed from Amsterdam April 8th, 1662. (Riker's History of Harlem, page 339).

Mr. Van Name is a member of the Holland Society of New York city. His mother is a Decker, which family is also one of he largest on the Island. She is Elizabeth, the only daughter of the late Benjamin Decker.

Mr. Van Name is a widower. His wife, Lizzie Emma, died May 14th, 1892. They had one child, Hazel Jane, now seven years old.

He is a large property owner in Northfield, and has long been identified with all movements of public benefit in that section. His knowledge of the Island and his numerous friends make him a strong man.

He was formerly a prominent Republican, serving for years on the county and state committees and in the county and state conventions. He was from time to time nominated for the different county offices including county judge, assembly and district-attorney, but always declined. He will not leave his large practice for public office.

He always expressed strong feelings against monopolies, and sincerely believing that they were fostered by the Republicans, in the fall of 1893 joined the Democratic party.

WILLIAM A. SUYDAM.

Mr. Suydam is the editor and publisher of the Staten Island *Gazette*, issued every Wednesday at Stapleton, and the *Sentinel*, every Saturday at New Brighton. He belongs to a Knickerbocker family, and the revolutionary records of Long Island and Brooklyn contain plentiful evidence of the patriotic activity of his ancestors. His father, James Suydam, established the first Democratic daily newspaper known in New York city, the *American Advocate*, which was published under the direction of James K. Polk, candidate for president.

About ten years ago, Mr. Suydam bought out the interest of Mr. Erastus Wiman in the Staten Island *Gazette* and *Sentinel*. He does a large business in stationery and printing supplies, and claims to own the most complete printing establishment on Staten Island. The Sentinel Printing House at New Brighton was built by Mr. Suydam, and a row of very pretty cottages at Rosebank, and others at Snug Harbor, represent some of his real estate investments.

CHARLES LIVINGSTON HUBBELL.

CHARLES LIVINGSTON HUBBELL.

CHARLES LIVINGSTON HUBBELL, son of Charles Wolcott Hubbell and Serena Hempsted, his wife, was born in Brooklyn, New York, July 14th, 1861. His great-grandfather, Philip Livingston, was one of the signers of the Declaration of Independence, and was a descendant of the Livingston family of Livingston Manor, New York, prominent in the early history of New York state.

Mr. Hubbell is descended on his father's side from Richard Hubbell, who came from Wales in 1645 and settled in Connecticut, and whose descendants were prominent officers in the revolutionary war, the war of 1812 and in the civil war.

Mr. Hubbell came to Staten Island when a boy of six years of age, and, after finishing an academic education, engaged in business for a few years, and then entered the law office of Hon. Frank Warner Angel, asst. United States district attorney, and commenced the study of law. He then attended the law school of New York University and was graduated in the class of '86, admitted to the bar May 12th, 1887, and entered into the practice of his profession with offices in New York city and on Staten Island.

Taking great interest in the development and prosperity of Staten Island, Mr. Hubbell formed the Granite Park Land and Improvement Company, of which he is president and counsel. He is also vice-regent of Staten Island Council, 1145, Royal Arcanum, charter member of Starin Hose Company, No. 5, of West New Brighton, charter member of the Republican Spellbinder Club of New York city, one of the founders of New York University Law Department Alumni Association, and member of the Irving Literary Society, which defeated all the famous and well-known debating societies in New York city and Brooklyn.

In addition, the popular and busy lawyer stumped the state for Harrison and Morton during that memorable campaign, and is active in politics and all that appertains to the welfare and prosperity of Richmond county.

He was married January 4th, 1893, to Eleanor Mathews Beach, and resides at West New Brighton, at which place he is engaged in the general practice of law, and has a growing and lucrative practice.

PERCIVAL G. ULLMAN.

Percival Glenroy Ullman was born at Tompkinsville May 29th, 1849, studied law with the Hon. Robert S. Hale (one of the regents of the University of New York) in Essex county, N. Y., and was admitted to the bar at Albany, in 1870. He is one of the best real estate lawyers in our county and is a close student to his large practice. He has been widely and prominently known for many years, and was the originator of the bill to remove the yellow fever burial grounds from Prince's Bay, the bill for relief of oyster planters now in congress, and is one of the directors of the first National Bank of St. George. He has also been prominent in numerous other beneficial, public and political movements in our county, and now resides at Huguenot.

Mr. Ullman was married January 18th, 1875, to Isabelle S., daughter of the late William Butcher. In 1878, he purchased his present residence at Huguenot, Staten Island, which he has since greatly enlarged and improved. Mr. and Mrs. Ullman have three children, two sons, Percy and Roscoe, and one daughter, Isabelle.

Mr. Ullman is of Knickerbocker stock and comes from one of the early, wealthy and influential Staten Island families. His mother's maiden name was Mary Louisa Corson who was born in the old family homestead on the Corson plantation, of which the Seamen's Retreat at Stapleton is part. She was also a granddaughter of Samuel Lockman, and a paternal granddaughter of Cornelius Corson.

Mr. Ullman is also a second cousin to the present admiral, E. A. K. Benham, of the United States Navy.

Clutes' History of Staten Island, page 401, speaks of the Lockman family as follows: This is one of the oldest Dutch families in the province. The first mentioned is Covert Lockman (sometimes called Lockerman) who arrived in America in 1633 in the Carvel St., Martyn. The New York civil list 1870 (see page 7) shows that Covert Lockman or Lockerman was one of the nine persons who represented the commonalty of New York and Brooklyn (since named) under the old Dutch government in 1647.

Abraham Lockman, a son of Covert Lockman, was the patentee of a large tract of land on Staten Island by Edmund Andros, governor-general of New York, in the reign of Charles 2nd, dated Sept. 12th, 1699. (See Liber "B" of deeds, page 341, county clerk's office.)

The Corson branch of the family dates back nearly as far as the Lockman. Clutes' History speaks of them as one of the wealthiest and most influential families of the Island, and Cornelius Corson is referred to in the records at Albany as a military captain, in 1687. (See page 358.)

This family also received a grant of a tract of 540 acres of land on Staten Island in the reign of Charles the 2nd, on Feb. 1st, 1687. (See Liber "B" of deeds, page 95, county clerk's office.

In 1712, in the reign of Queen Ann, Cornwalace Bowman conveyed to Christian Corson, gentleman, another large tract of land. (See Liber "C" of deeds, page 51.)

Cornelius Corson's will was probated in the county of Richmond in 1793, and among others he left a son named Christian Corson who is spoken of as second judge and lieutenant colonel, in 1742.

Richard Corson represented Richmond county in the legislatures of 1816, 1817 and 1818. (See civil list 1870.)

JAMES L. BARGER.

JAMES L. BARGER, eldest son of Henry Barger, was born on Staten Island, December 12th, 1868. He entered the law school of Columbia College in 1889, where he enjoyed the advantage of a thorough legal training under the tuition of the late Professor Theodore W. Dwight, during the last years of his connection with the law department of that institution. He was admitted as attorney and counselor of the supreme court, in May 1862, and was graduated one month later with the degree of L. L. B., *cum laude*.

He at once entered upon a general practice of the law with an office at No. 2 Wall st., New York. He has been signally successful in the management of his clients' interests, and is already enjoying a comparatively lucrative and gowing practice.

Mr. Barger is one of the young men of Staten Island whose history is all before them, but should he live to fulfill the promise of his young and vigorous manhood, it will not be many years before he will have a place among the foremost lawyers of Richmond county.

CORONER WHITMAN.

STEPHEN E. WHITMAN, M. D.

Dr. Stephen E. Whitman, younger son of Stephen Whitman, of Port Richmond, was born in New York city in 1855. The family moved to Port Richmond in 1862, into the house on the corner of Broadway and Bennett street, where they still reside.

In 1876, Mr. Whitman began the study of medicine with Dr. W. C. Walser. After being graduated, in 1881, from the College of Physicians and Surgeons, Dr. Whitman spent two or three years in Bellevue, St. Vincent and Chambers street hospitals, and then practiced with his former tutor, remaining for a long time as his assistant. He next moved to Brooklyn, where he practiced for five years. At the end of that period, he returned to the Island and opened an office in Port Richmond, where he has built up a large practice.

In the election of 1891, Dr. Whitman was elected coroner on the Democratic ticket in opposition to Dr. J. Walter Wood. He has had many important cases during his official term, the last of which was the killing of Adam Frelich by Officer Wells of the Richmond county police, the officer being exonerated by the jury.

The Whitman family came from England prior to 1680 and settled in Weymouth, Mass., and from the coat of arms of the family, it is evident that they belonged to the aristocracy and nobility.

Dr. Whitman's father, Capt. Stephen Whitman, commanded several famous Liverpool packets and the vessels of the old New York Mail S. S. Co., and later of the Cromwell line to New Orleans.

During the war of the rebellion Capt. Whitman was chased by the famous privateer Alabama, but, fortunately escaped. He has been a member of the Produce Exchange for the past fifteen years, and is a member of the Marine Society. He was trustee of the village of Port Richmond for seventeen years, and since 1873 has been inspector of storage under the name of Whitman & Fisher.

Dr. Whitman's mother was Miss Maria Robertson Dean, of Deansville, Conn., of one of the oldest and most prominent families in that part of the state.

The doctor, who is still unmarried, lives and has his office in the family residence at Port Richmond, where he is esteemed a skillful physician, a faithful and competent county official and a popular member of society.

GEORGE W. STAKE.

GEORGE W. STAKE was born at Stapleton, Staten Island in 1869, and was educated at the German and the public schools, and at the College of the City of New York, New York city. He was graduated from said college with honors in 1887, receiving the degree of A. B. In 1889, he was graduated from the Columbia Law School with the degree of L. L. B., *cum laude*, and from the Department of Political Science with the degree of A. M. In 1890, he passed examination in the same college and received the degree of Ph. D. He was admitted to the bar in 1891, and is now practicing the profession of law with offices at Stapleton and at 59 Liberty street, New York. Mr. Stake is counsel of the town board of Middletown and Staten Island counsel of the Anglo-American Loan and Savings Association. He is a member of the German Association, Erheiterung, of Stapleton, the Delta Kappa Epsilon Club of 435 5th avenue, New York city, and a member of secret orders. Mr. Stake is unmarried and lives at Stapleton.

CORNELIUS SHEA.

CORNELIUS SHEA was born at Richmond Valley, S. I., in May 1863, just one week after the battle of Chancelorsville, and was named after his uncle who was killed in that battle. In 1887, he removed to Tottenville and has, ever since, been a resident of that village.

Mr. Shea, is a story writer or author by profession, and has been for five years a regular contributor to *Golden Hours*, a young people's weekly, published by Norman L. Munro, of New York city, a paper of very extensive circulation. His stories have been honored by some of the finest and most prominent illustrations of those of any contributor of *Golden Hours*, and have always taken a high rank; always being of the most entertaining and exciting character.

Mr. Shea, who is somewhat of a politician, as well as an author, is always prominent in the local contests in his town, and has twice been elected town clerk on the Democratic ticket, when nearly every other candidate was defeated. Mr. Shea is also an enthusiastic club and secret society man, and is a member of Huguenot Lodge, F. & A. M., Richmond Lodge, K. of P., Bentley Lodge, I. O. of O. F., of Tottenville, of Eureka Engine Co. No. 2, of Tottenville, and the Staten Island Press Club.

JOHN WIDDECOMBE.

JOHN WIDDECOMBE, eldest son of John Widdecombe, and his wife Helen, née Doyle, was born in London, England, Oct. 29th, 1856. When eight years of age, he was entered in St. Charles' College, founded by the late Cardinal Manning. At the age of fifteen years, he passed the preliminary examination prescribed by the rules of the Incorporated Law Society, and a year later was articled to William H. Tattam, a London solicitor, for a period of five years. In 1877, he was admitted as a solicitor of the supreme court of judicature, in England.

In 1875, he was commissioned as second lieutenant in Her Majesty's auxiliary forces (5 Essex Rifle Volunteers) retiring in 1881 with the rank of captain.

He practiced his profession in London, from 1877 to 1882, when he came to New York bringing letters of introduction to the late Cardinal McCloskey and other prominent persons in New York city. Soon after his arrival he entered the law office of Holt & Butler as managing clerk, and in 1887, upon the motion of Wm. Allen Butler, president of the New York Bar Association, seconded by the recommendation of such prominent lawyers as Abram Cole, Wm. B. Hornblower and others, he was admitted as attorney and counselor-at-law, in the state of New York.

In 1888, he removed to Stapleton, Staten Island, and the following year, after a brief co-partnership with ex-Judge J. J. McKeon, he began the practice of the law on his own account, occupying an office with Messrs. Holt & Butler. From that time his practice has steadily increased, so that at the present time he is regarded as one of the most successful and prominent members of the Richmond county bar, and he now occupies a handsome suite of offices in the Savings Bank building in Stapleton.

In 1890, he assisted the Hon. Geo. Gallagher, then district-attorney, in the prosecution of the celebrated election fraud cases, and in 1891, he assisted District-Attorney Fitzgerald in the Emmons murder case. In both instances he received many warm commendations for the thoroughness with which he prepared the case and the ability and skill displayed in presenting the facts to the court and jury.

On October 1st, 1879, he married Margaret, second daughter of G. T. W. Mugliston, M. D., of the Elms, Enfield.

Mr. and Mrs. Widdecombe have three children: Lawrence Winstanley, aged twelve, a student at St. Austin's school, Arthur Bernard, aged eleven, a student at the Staten Island Academy, and Emma Marguerite, aged three.

THE LATE EPHRAIM J. TOTTEN

EPHRAIM J. TOTTEN was born March 30th, 1806, at the homestead near Bethel Church, Tottenville. During his early life, from 1823 to 1845, he followed the sea, being captain and owner or part owner of various vessels engaged in the coasting trade. In 1850, he took a load of merchandise to the Pacific coast and engaged for some time in mercantile pursuits. Although he met with some reverses in sending his goods on a long and perilous voyage, he did, on the whole, a prosperous business during his short stay in California.

On his return to Staten Island he carried on a mercantile business in Tottenville until 1874, when he retired from business and began the cultivation of his farm, the old homestead property.

Mr. Totten was always known as an energetic, enterprising, public-spirited citizen, and held a number of public offices. He was supervisor in 1846-7 and was a member of the legislature in 1848. He was one of the projectors of the Staten Island railroad and one of the directors.

When he was 40 years of age he became a church member and from that time his life was devoted to church work, and all its interests were his. He filled every office and was recording steward and president of the board of trustees of Bethel M. E. Church for nearly 40 years, holding these offices up to the time of his death in April 1891.

He raised a family of eight children, six of whom are still living. He was born on the place where his father, grandfather and great grandfather lived since the Revolutionary. The old homestead stood in front of the present house. In 1855, he pulled down the old one and erected that which now stands just back of the old site. The old farm occupied nearly the whole village of Tottenville which took its name after him and his brothers.

DR. R. HENRY GOLDER.

DR. R. HENRY GOLDER.

ROBERT HENRY GOLDER, M. D., has been a resident and practising physician at Rossville since 1849. He was born in Philadelphia, Pa., Sept. 23rd, 1820. His father, John Golder, was born in Annapolis, Md., May 23rd, 1783. His paternal ancestry dates back for two or more generations before that period and in that locality, and were of German descent. His mother, whose maiden name was Johnson, also descended from an old Maryland family. Her brother, Hon. John Johnson, was chancellor of Maryland in the early part of this century, under whom John Golder studied law. Senator Reverdy Johnson, who was also U. S. minister to England, and cousin of John Golder, studied law under his father and also Chief Justice Taney of U. S. supreme court.

John Golder was district-attorney for two counties on the eastern shore of Maryland before the war of 1812. In July of that year, he was married to Margaret McMaken of Philadelphia, to which city he removed in 1814, and practiced his profession until 1840, when he removed with his family to New York city, where he died March 21st, 1864. He had four children: Julia A., Sarah M., John J. and Robert H., the subject of this sketch.

Margaret McMaken, the mother of Dr. Golder, was born in Philadelphia and died in New York, March 9th, 1864. She was of Scotch-Irish descent. Her mother's family, the Scotts, who were nearly allied to the family of Sir Walter Scott, came to this country about the middle of the last century and settled mostly in Bucks county, Pa., where the "Scott Memorial Church" and "Scott's Manor" still stand. But two descendants of this branch of the family are living.

In 1839, Dr. Golder began the study of pharmacy and afterward was in business as a druggist. After a preparatory course under Prof. Valentine Mott and John S. Whittaker, he entered the medical department of the University of the City of New York, from which he was graduated in 1846.

He was married to Catharine V. Dunham, of New Brunswick, N. J., in December 1847. Of their four children, Valentine Mott, Annette, Reverdy J., and Margaret D., the latter is the only surviving one.

DR. DAVID M. COLEMAN.

DAVID M. COLEMAN, M. D., was born in Springfield, Mass., on July 4th, 1849, and the early part of his life was spent on a farm, and attending public and private schools.

In 1869, he moved to Dutchess county, N. Y., and attended Dr. Hoyt's private academy for two years. In 1875, he began the study of medicine, and in 1881, he entered the New York Homœopathic Medical College, from which he was graduated in the spring of 1884.

During the last year of his college course, the doctor was appointed visiting physician to the Wilson Mission School for Infants, corner 8th street and Avenue A. He was also appointed visiting physician to the New York Dispensary, 23rd street and 3rd avenue, and was assistant to Prof. Thompson, in surgery. Two days in the week he had a private clinic in the Dispensary.

At the close of 1884, Dr. Coleman moved to Tottenville, in which place he still resides and has a large and growing practice. In 1893, he was elected health officer.

Dr. Coleman is one of the most respected and useful members of the profession and has a host of friends who rejoice in his success.

J. WALTER WOOD, A. M., M .D.

One of the most prominent and successful physicians and surgeons of Staten Island is Dr. J. Walter Wood, who was born at Mariners' Harbor, Apr. 23rd, 1856. He is a descendant of the Dongan family. His education was thorough in both the academic and medical schools. His gentlemanly manners and great skill soon brought him a large and lucrative practice.

Dr. Wood was health officer, for a number of years, of the town of Northfield and the village of Port Richmond, and coroner for the county, and was esteemed one of the most efficient officials of the county.

Dr. Wood is a $32°$ Mason and is a Past Master of Richmond Lodge, Past High Priest of Tyrian Chapter, Surgeon to York Commandery, a Noble of Mecca Shrine, and for several years was president of the S. I. Masonic Mutual Benefit Association and is examining physician for the North Western Masonic Insurance Company.

He is Past Chancellor of S. I. Lodge Knights of Pythias, and examining physician for the Odd Fellows, Workingmen, Foresters, Legion of Honor, Templars of Liberty, and the New York Life Insurance Company.

Dr. Wood is visiting surgeon to the S. R. Smith Infirmary, and president of the Port Richmond branch of the Co-operative Building Bank of New York.

DR. E. A. HERVEY.

EDWIN A. HERVEY, M. D.

EDWIN ADDISON HERVEY was born at South Durham, N. Y., January 16th, 1824. He is the third son of the late D. B. Hervey, ex-assemblyman from Greene county. His early education was received in the public schools and from private tutors. At the age of seventeen he was asked to teach the district school in his native town, in which capacity he continued there and elsewhere in the county for a period of five years. He then went to Ellenville, Ulster county, where he acted as clerk and book-keeper in a store and tannery for two years.

In 1848, he came to Staten Island and engaged as teacher in Westfield, remaining eight years. During the last six of these he resided with Dr. E. W. Hubbard, from whom he received his preparatory course of medical instruction. He then entered the University Medical College of New York city, from which he was graduated in 1859, receiving the valuable Elliot prize for skill in anatomy.

Dr. Hervey located in Rossville, where he still continues to practice. He has been especially successful as an obstetrician. He has been physician to St. Michael's Home, Greenridge, since its establishment. Though never active in politics, he has been a coroner of Richmond county for eighteen years, the last five terms having been successive.

Dr. Hervey has been twice married. His first wife was Eliza J., daughter of John Williams, of Rossville; his second, Grace E., daughter of T. W. C. Moore, for many years Queen's Messenger between New York and Washington. To the latter were born two children: Charles Edwin, who died in infancy, and William Addison.

SUPT. O. H. HOAG.

ORRY HUESTED HOAG, superintendent of the Union Free school at Port Richmond, was born at Pleasant Plains, this county, Feb. 17th, 1857. The education of his boyhood was received in the public schools of the town of Westfield. At an early age, he left school and clerked for several years in different stores of the village. In the winter of '75 and '76, he took the theoretical course in Eastman's Business College, at Poughkeepsie, N. Y.

A vacancy in the primary department of the public school of his native village was filled by his appointment, Oct. 18th, 1876, in which position he continued till June 1880, when he resigned to more properly pursue his studies and prepare himself for his chosen calling, by taking the classical course at the state Normal school, at Geneseo, N. Y. Graduating in 1884, he was elected to the principalship of Castleton Corners public school, Staten Island. In the spring of 1890, he resigned to take the principalship of his present school, becoming superintendent in the following year.

In his profession, Mr. Hoag is painstaking, effective in discipline, and devoted, not using it as a stepping stone to something else.

BENJAMIN H. WARFORD.

CAPT. BENJAMIN H. WARFORD, youngest son of Charles Warford, was born in the city of Troy, N. Y., Oct. 11th, 1831. When nineteen years of age, he was captain of a vessel, and at twenty-one, the owner, and from that time his business has steadily increased, until now the firm of Warford & Andrews, of which Mr. Warford is manager and the largest owner, have one of the most numerous fleets of barges doing business in New York harbor, with offices in New York and West Troy.

At the beginning of the war, Capt. Warford raised a company of volunteers and went to the front as second lieutenant. He was engaged in fourteen battles, and on June 30th, 1862, was promoted to the rank of captain, for gallant conduct.

Capt. Warford is a Republican of the "stalwart" kind, and has always been active in politics and a liberal contributor to the cause of his party. He has served one year as vice-chairman of the county General Committee and has been its chairman for four years, but declined re-election last spring.

He headed the Blaine electoral ticket in 1884, and was one of the delegates to the national convention at Chicago, in 1892, and he helped to make the famous fight for James G. Blaine in that convention.

CROWELL M. SEGUINE.

CROWELL M. SEGUINE, founder of Giffords-by-the-Sea, was born at the old homestead near Giffords, March 9th, 1851. He is descended in a direct line from the early Huguenot family of that name that settled on the Island nearly two hundred years ago.

Mr. Seguine has always been a successful and enterprising business man, and more than any other has contributed to the growth of his native place. He is a large land owner and conducts a successful real estate and coal business.

He married in 1886, Josephine, daughter of Charles A. Canavello, of Giffords, by whom he has two children, twin daughters, Louisa and Rosa, aged three years.

Mr. Seguine has always been an active, earnest Republican but never has entered politics as an office seeker, preferring to build up his private business and promote the growth of the village founded by him, and his business interests. He has been always known as an honest upright business man, and he and his family are held in high esteem among a large circle of friends.

FRANK L. HADKINS

FRANK L. HADKINS, one of the well-known businessmen of Tottenville, was born in Perth Amboy, N. J., in 1863, and is the youngest child of the late John H. Hadkins.

The same year, Mr. Hadkins established with Chas. Low, the bottling business in Perth Amboy, but, owing to a lack of suitable supply of water, Mr. Hadkins purchased the interest of Mr. Low in 1867 and removed the plant to Tottenville where he continued the business until his death in 1872, when he was succeeded by his son Robert H., then seventeen years of age. The son carried on the business and largely increased it with the assistance of his brother, Frank the subject of this sketch. The latter became a partner in the business in 1887, and the brothers built the large factory under the name of R. H. Hadkins & Bro.

Upon the death of Robert in 1889, Frank took charge of the business and has since conducted it under the name and style of the Hadkins Bottling Co., the firm consisting of Mrs. Mary H. and Frank L. Hadkins. The business has steadily increased until the establishment is now the largest for carbonated beverages on the Island, and Mr. Hadkins does the largest business of the kind on the Island or in the suburbs of New York.

In 1888, Mr. Hadkins was elected to the office of excise commissioner to fill a vacancy, and was re-elected in 1890 and held the office until it was abolished in 1892 and a board of county commissioners appointed.

In 1887, he married Annie L., only daughter of S. Webb Hopping. Mr. and Mrs. Hadkins have one child, Marion L., aged 4 years.

REUBEN SIMONSON.

REUBEN SIMONSON, son of George and Mary Simonson, was born at Kreischerville, Jan 11th, 1850. His mother, whose maiden name was Johnson, was a descendant of an old Staten Island family of that name.

Mr. Simonson is engaged with Capt. Peter Androvette in the towing business, and is part owner of three tugs, George B. Roe, Allie and Evie.

In 1873, he married Fannie E., daughter of Charles and Susan Androvette, of Kreischerville, and has two children living, Cyrennius, aged eighteen years, and Evaline, aged fourteen.

Mr. Simonson has always been looked upon as one of the solid enterprising business men of Kreischerville, and has been held in high esteem by all who know him socially or who have had business dealings with him.

CAPT. JOHN M. ANDROVETTE.

CAPT. JOHN M. ANDROVETTE, the eldest son of the late Peter Androvette, was born in Kreischerville in 1831. His grandfather, Charles, was one of the original settlers in Kreischerville, and owned a large farm, which comprised nearly all the land on which the present village is built.

On December 5th, 1852, Capt. Androvette married Elizabeth Worth, who died in 1876, leaving two daughters, Mrs. Alfred Mersereau, living in Tottenville, and Miss Clara S., still living with her father, and one son, Reuben W.

In 1878, he married Elizabeth, daughter of Wm. Joline, of Tottenville, by whom he has one daughter, Bessie, now at school.

Capt. Androvette has always followed the water, beginning as early as 1857, as part owner and captain of the "Fire-brick," engaged in transporting fire-brick for B. Kreischer & Nephew.

Mr. Androvette has been a prominent member of Bethel Church for the last thirty years, and during twenty-eight years of that time he has been a member of the official board and a licensed exhorter, and is now district steward, treasurer of the Sunday-school, and custodian of all collections for benevolent purposes.

REV. FREDERICK BLOOM.

THE subject of this sketch, Rev. Frederick Bloom, was born Sept. 12th, 1852, near Everittstown, Hunterdon county, N. J.

His early life was spent on a farm, but at the age of eighteen he went to Quakertown, N. J. A series of revival services was held in the village, and among the large number of converts was Frederick Bloom. He then felt called upon to preach, and, by the help of friends, he succeeded in entering Pennington Seminary, and remained there for nearly a year. He then took up school teaching and soon after married Miss Lizzie Hoffman.

Still he was dissatisfied. His great ambition was to preach. At that time he was teaching school in Centreville, N. J., and he was appointed to fill the charge at that place. This he continued to do for two years, and in 1874, he was admitted to conference. While stationed at Denville in 1884, Mr. Bloom took the full course at Drew Theological Seminary, and finished with the post graduate course.

In 1891, Mr. Bloom was appointed pastor of Bethel M. E. Church, Tottenville, where his labors have met with much success.

BETHEL CHURCH, TOTTENVILLE.

Bethel Church was first erected on the present site in 1841. It was a frame building 40x50 feet and was dedicated in the spring of 1841 by Charles Pitman; then presiding elder of the district. In 1885, about $3,000 was spent in improving and decorating the church. The congregation, however, did not long enjoy the benefit of their labors and sacrifices; for on January 10th, 1886, the church took fire and was burned to the ground.

Not disheartened by their loss the congregation immediately went to work and erected the present handsome new brick structure, which was dedicated May 8th, 1887, by Bishop Harris. The church as it now stands cost about $20,000.

ST. PATRICK'S CHURCH, RICHMOND.

ST. PATRICK'S CHURCH.

St. Patrick's Parish was cared for by the priests of Clifton and Rossville, and the services were held in private houses and halls until 1862, when the Rev. John Barry, of Rossville, built the substantial brick church on Garretson st. Lawrence Searers and John Gonond were elected the first trustees.

The mission remained in care of Rossville until 1884, when Rev. John Coffee was appointed pastor, who resided at St. Stephen's Home, New Dorp.

In 1886, he was succeeded by the present rector who instantly set to work to procure a parsonage, and purchased the large brick house adjoining the church—built and at one time occupied by Judge John G. Vaughn. This rectory is now wholly free from debt, in thorough repair and well furnished at a total cost of $7,000.

The church likewise was improved and beautified at an expense of $2,000, whilst its original debt of $3,000 has been lowered to $2,000, and through the organized effort of a church debt society will soon be wholly cleared. For this result of seven years' labor, the rector has to thank his innumerable friends of all denominations throughout Richmond county and New York city.

It is computed that within the parish limits from Eltingville to Garretsons there are 500 Roman Catholics.

REV. JAMES PATRICK BYRNES.

REV. JAMES PATRICK BYRNES was born Jan. 6th, 1854, in County Limerick, Ireland. He came to New York city in April 1870, and in September 1871, entered St. Charles' College, Maryland; was ordained at St. Joseph's Seminary, Troy, N. Y., and was immediately assigned to duty in the Church of the Immaculate Conception in 14th street, New York, where he remained until 1883, when he was transferred to Sing Sing, and in 1886, he was made pastor of St. Patrick's Church, Richmond

REV. C. F. HULL.

REV. CHARLES F. HULL, pastor of St. Paul's M. E. Church, Tottenville, was born in New York city, April 28th, 1842, and was graduated from the 13th street public school in 1855. He was converted in 1860, and was baptized in the Antioch Baptist Church by the Rev. J. Q. Adams. In 1861, he enlisted in the 5th N. Y. Vols. (Duryeas' Zouaves), and served with that regiment in the Army of the Potomac. In 1864, he received a commission in the navy, and remained in the service until after the fall of Richmond. He then entered Madison (now Colgate) University, and spent four years in study. In 1869, he married Miss Mattie Boyd, of Hamilton, N. Y., and was ordained pastor of the Baptist church in Beekman, N. Y. In 1872, he returned to the University, entered the Theological Seminary, and was graduated with the class of 1873.

The same year he was called to the pastorate of the Baptist church in Northville, N. Y. In 1875, the Mariners' Harbor, S. I., Baptist church invited him to become their pastor, and he remained with them until 1877, when, on account of change in denominational views, he applied for admission, and was received, into the Newark Conference of the Methodist Episcopal church. Since that date his appointments have been as follows: 1877, Mt. Hope, N. J.; 1878-80, Woodrow, S. I.; 1881, Otisville, N. Y.; 1882-84, Rockland Lake, N. Y.; 1885-87, Bayonne, N. J.; 1888-90, Rahway, N. J. In 1891 he was appointed to St. Paul's, Tottenville, of which church he still remains the pastor.

ST. PETER'S CHURCH, KREISCHERVILLE.

REV. JACOB J. GANSS.

Rev. Jacob J. Ganss was born in the city of Frankfort-on-the-Main, Aug. 3rd, 1859. Before entering the ministry he studied medicine three and a half years, after which he studied theology in Germany and Switzerland. He came to this country in 1881, and took a position in Hoboken, N. J., as a teacher of mathematics and languages, in the Martha Institute, for one year.

On the first Sunday in Advent, in 1882, Mr. Ganss preached his first sermon in Kreischerville, and his zeal for the welfare of the congregation attracted the attention at once of the officers of St. Peter's Church, and pointed him out as a fit successor to the Rev. Dr. Mohn, the first pastor of the Kreischerville church.

After having passed a most satisfactory examination, he was, by recommendation of the Honorable Classis, of New York, ordained as minister of the Gospel, June 13th, 1883, and duly installed as minister of the German Evangelical Church — St. Peter's — of Kreischerville. The church has steadily grown in members, influence and good works under Mr. Ganss' ministration, until now it is one of the most prosperous in Westfield.

REV. D. B. F. RANDOLPH

REV. D. B. F. RANDOLPH.

Rev. D. B. F. Randolph is the pastor of Trinity Methodist Episcopal Church, Richmond Terrace, West New Brighton, which has a capacity of about seven hundred sittings, an exceptionally large and beautiful parsonage, and a membership of about three hundred persons, who are warmly attached to all its interests and contribute generously to its support and to all the benevolent objects of the church at large. Their present pastor is now serving them for the fifth year under the new time limit of the denomination.

Mr. Randolph was born in Newark, N. J., in 1848, attended the grammar and high schools of that city, and was graduated from Pennington Seminary in 1868 and from Drew Theological Seminary, with the degree of Bachelor of Divinity, in 1871. In the latter institution he enjoyed the privilege of sitting under the instruction of Drs. McClintock, Foster, Strong, Buttz and Nadal.

In the spring of 1871, he was received into the Newark annual conference, and, in the order of the church, after four years of conference studies, was ordained elder in 1875.

In the economy of Methodism, Mr. Randolph has been the pastor of several churches, more recently at Hoboken, Perth Amboy, Newark and Hackettstown.

EX-SHERIFF MARSH.

ISAAC M. MARSH was born in Essex county, N. J., in 1821. When twenty-two years of age he came to Staten Island and established a carriage-making business in Richmond, where for many years he carried on the largest business of the kind in the county. He was serving as deputy-sheriff at the time the present jail was built and was deputy under Sheriffs Simonson, Dissosway (two terms) Guyon, Ellis and Lockman, and one term as sheriff. About the time of the beginning of the war he was elected president of the Union Condensed Milk Co., of Orange county.

At this time Peter V. Nolan, who had been in his employ for many years, was made a partner in the business, and Mr. Marsh moved to Orange county where he remained for three years. After his return to Richmond he was appointed police commissioner and held the office for twelve years. He was also one of the Southfield drainage commissioners and one of the appraisors for the B. & O. extension.

During the war Mr. Marsh furnished about seven thousand horses and other supplies for the army.

Mr. Marsh is now living quietly at Richmond and still retains his interest in the carriage business as senior partner of the firm of Marsh & Nolan.

NATHANIEL JARVIS WYETH

NATHANIEL JARVIS WYETH, son of Charles and Elizabeth Norris Wyeth, was born in Baltimore, Md., under the star of the Democratic thirties of the nineteenth century. He was schooled at Mount Hope in that city, and at the classical high school of Laurenceville, N. J., and was graduated from the college and law school of Harvard University, a student from 1846 to 1852, both included.

The Wyeth family was divided in colonial times, one branch settling in Massachusetts and the other in Virginia. George Wyeth represented the latter, having participated in the Declaration of Independence, beside being chief architect of the constitution of the United States.

Nathaniel Wyeth was named after his distinguished and valiant uncle, Nathaniel Jarvis Wyeth, of Cambridge, Mass., who crossed the American continent in the early thirties and settled in Oregon. After his return to his home, he became the largest ice harvestter, horticulturist, brick maker and inventor and aboriginal linguist in the country, as Schoolcroft's work testifies.

Mr. Wyeth began to practice law in the city of New York in January 1853. His first memorable suit involved the title to the Wilson survey of sixty thousand acres in Virginia, with the eminent Josiah Randall as his opponent, and was successful. This gave him great eclat in wild land law, which he has sustained. Then followed the Jacob Wyeth will matter of Cambridge, Mass., assisted by the Hon. B. R. Curtis. In 1856, Albert Journeay, Edward Banker, Frederick R. Grote, Stephen Seguine and other enterprising residents of Staten Island, employed Mr. Wyeth as counsel for the construction of the lethargic Staten Island railroad, which became an operated road and earned attractive dividends soon after.

In 1856, Mr. Wyeth organized with Col. Henry S. Lansing and Prof. Morse, the People's Oil and Mining Company of West Virginia, with $2,000,000 capital. As assemblyman of the New York legislature of 1867 he was on committee of colleges, academies and common schools and the sub-committee of the whole. He there advocated and passed the original elevated railroad act for the real projectors of rapid transit in New York, Messrs. Harvey and Jennings; also the East river bridge bill for his client, John A. Roebling. He addressed the house on the constitutional amendment, enlargement of the canal locks, removal of the quarantine and the Metropolitan harbor district, the forerunner of greater New York. All these speeches were published by the hundreds and were disseminated for their worth.

In 1868, Mr. Wyeth drew the papers for the first petroleum railroad in the oil regions of Pennsylvania, to the great profit of the projectors, George H. Bissell, Miller and others. He likewise prepared the patent papers for Col. Roberts' oil torpedo and aided in sustaining them in the interference proceedings which culminated in revolutionizing oil production, and making the gallant colonel very wealthy.

In 1870, at the solicitation of Harlon M. Wilcox, of Buffalo, Mr. Wyeth gave much attention to the passage of the Arcade railroad bill of New York. The same year he originated, prepared and passed the Staten Island bridge and harbor improvement bill, which received the cordial approbation of the foremost engineers and scientists, James Hall, Harlon M. Wilcox, Wm. J. McAlpin, Albert C. Stimers, C. Delafield, Washington Roebling and others, Mr. Roebling writing "a great desideratum and the only practical scheme to accomplish this result." He also, that year, projected and obtained an act for a general commercial institution to be operated in Bureaux for the different kinds of business.

The following year, 1871, as chairman of the committee on transportation and inter-communication of the Richmond County Improvement Company, Lawyer Wyeth was the author of their famous January report. The same year, he labored about a month at Trenton, while the New Jersey legislature was in session, to procure the passage of his New Jersey Tube Transporation Company bill, by which the corporators obtained a franchise to construct railroads in New Jersey, thus breaking the monopoly of the Pennsylvania railroad, and helped to secure the passage of the general railroad act of that state.

Three years later, Mr. Wyeth introduced through Richmond county's then able assemblyman, Hon. Stephen D. Stephens, Jr., his Belt Railroad Improvement Company bill, with the object of reclaiming all the outlying marshes and meadows of the county and presenting to his fellow-citizens the finest beaches, purest airs and most attractive homes and most pleasant public resorts in the country. The previous two years were somewhat engaged in assisting Chief Engineer Abbott in securing terminal facilities for the Continental Railway Company to New York city through the New Jersey Tube Transportation Company.

In 1880, Mr. Wyeth argued successfully at length
against the construction of the act of that year to
facilitate the collection of taxes for state purposes,
that would exempt corporations from taxes for local
purposes (which was nine-tenths of the gross tax) before
that eminent jurist, Jasper T. Gilbert, in Brooklyn
at a special term, and won. About this time Counselor
Wyeth became general counsel for the universal inventor,
James Montgomery, of Philadelphia, and continued
such till the death of Mr. Montgomery.

Beside originating, projecting and counseling such
generally useful measures, the subject of this sketch
pursues a systematic course of jurisprudence, science
and literature in his select and capacious library at
his "Florence home" and office on Richmond Hill, engaging
in many cases at the bar of this county and
elsewhere. His regular office was near Wall street,
New York.

Progress and humanity are the emblems of his
realization.

JOHN L. YOUNG.

EX-JUSTICE JOHN L. YOUNG was born in London, England, in 1818, served his time in London as carriage painter, and came to America in 1852. He arrived in New York on Monday, and the following day obtained a situation at Rahway, N. J., which was then a centre of the carriage business.

He remained in one factory seventeen years, and in 1869, he moved to Richmond and has been in the employ of Isaac March and Marsh & Nolan since that time. He is now living in comfortable circumstances.

In 1881, Mr. Young was elected justice and held the office for eight years. He was also district clerk and trustee of Richmond school for eighteen years. He married, in 1838, Miss Emma Harris, daughter of the famous aeronaut, Thos. Harris. She died in Rahway in 1856 and was buried on the anniversary of her marriage.

In 1858, he married Miss Susan Harrington, of New York, who is still living. Mr. and Mrs. Young have three daughters, Mrs. Wm. Finley, Mrs. George Hatfield, of Rahway, and Mrs. George Lewis, of Jersey City, sixteen grandchildren and five great grandchildren.

SUPPLEMENT.

1894.

R. W. POLLOCK.

R. W. POLLOCK, General Traffic Agent of the Staten Island Rapid Transit Railroad Company, was born in Pittsburgh, Pa. He entered railway service Nov. 11th, 1872, since which time he has been consecutively to June 1st, 1873, receiving clerk of the local freight station Allegheny Valley Railroad at Pittsburgh, Pa.; June 1st, 1873, to spring of 1876, chief clerk local freight department of the same road; spring of 1876 to April 1879, clerk in general freight agent's office of the same road, and April 1879 to August 15th, 1883, chief clerk of the same office, same road; August 15th, 1883, to Dec. 1st, 1885, General Agent Rochester and Pittsburgh Railroad at Pittsburgh; Dec. 1st, 1885, to Oct. 1st, 1886, General Agent Buffalo, New York and Pittsburgh Railroad, same city; October 1st, 1886, to date, General Traffic Agent Staten Island Rapid Transit Railroad, New York.

JUSTICE VAUGHN.

JOHN G. VAUGHN, justice of the peace of the town of Southfield, was born in Ireland. He came to America in 1847, lived in New York a while, then moved to New Jersey, then to Williamsburg, at which place he learned the trade of mason and builder.

In 1849, Mr. Vaughn moved to Staten Island and worked at his trade on R. Hamilton's first building erected in Hamilton Park. His next move was to Richmond, where he became a partner with Builder Burbank of Rossville. After the dissolution of the firm, Mr. Vaughn carried on the business in his own name, and among other buildings erected by him are the public school-house at Tompkinsville, the Tully buildings, school-houses Nos. 2 and 3 of Southfield, the Roman Catholic church and parsonage at Richmond and the county clerk's office at Richmond.

Through his aid a bill was passed in the legislature to purchase the ground for the village of Edgewater Park, which he had built for the trustees of the park.

While he was living at Richmond the boundary line of the town of Southfield included the greater part of what is now known as the town of Middletown. Prior to this there were but four towns in Richmond county, and on one occasion a tie was found in the board, caused by Col. Ray Tompkins and the Hon. Richard Christopher of Castleton, each claiming the seat of supervisor representing Castleton. Hon. Robert Christy, Hon. H. Weed and John G. Vaughn went to Albany and had the town of Middletown created out of the towns of Southfield and Castleton.

In 1858, John G. Vaughn was elected justice of the peace, a position he holds up to this date.

In 1862, he raised a company of Staten Islanders and went to the front with Gen. Banks' army in the West. Mr. Vaughn and his company rendered good service and were engaged in all the battles up to the taking of Port Hudson, at which time he resigned and returned home to his family then residing at Vanderbilt's Landing. The next spring he was re-elected justice and the following autumn was nominated and elected for the office of one of the three county superintendents of the poor.

In politics he is a sterling Democrat and has secured great influence in his party. He has been delegate to the county conventions for over thirty years, has been to senatorial, congressional and state conventions during all that period and nominated, at Jamaica, the Hon. Erastus Brooks as member of the last constitutional convention. He was elected three times in succession to the office of chairman of the county committee and held this position in 1884, when, it is well known, he most ably aided in the election of President Cleveland. The facts in the case are these: The night of the election Mr. Vaughn, as previously arranged, after carefully canvassing the vote of Richmond county, telegraphed to the Democratic headquarters to the Hon. M. C. Murphy and Hon. James Smith who had charge at the Hoffman House, New York, that Richmond county had given for Cleveland 1892 majority.

When the canvass of the state was by them completed, awaiting the official returns, they discovered that the state of New York had been won by the Republicans. The committee sent for Mr. Vaughn, to whom they stated that the result of the national ticket devolved on Staten Island; that, as was the fact, it required the vote of New York to elect and it required the vote of Staten Island to overcome Blaine's majority, Blaine having a majority of all the votes cast in this state down to the battery, of 923. On the final canvass of the Staten Island vote, Cleveland had received a plurality of 1970 overcoming Blaine's vote by 1047 majority of thirty, giving to the nation a Democratic president.

JOHN B. NEWHALL, M. E.

John B. Newhall, eldest son of Morris B. Newhall, was born in the year 1855 at Randolph, Mass.

When very young his family moved to South Boston, at which place his early school training began. As a boy he manifested a great taste for mechanics, and as soon as his age would permit, he entered the technical school, taking a thorough course in hydraulic and mechanical engineering.

About this time, he suffered an affliction in the loss of his parents, and being thrown on his own resources, he secured a position with the Boston Machine Co. After a few years of experience and untiring energy, he was advanced and put in charge of the water pipe, valve and hydrant department.

In this manner, he became interested in water-works engineering, and in 1888 was made general superintendent of the Maine Water Co., which owned and operated seven separate water-works plants in different cities and towns in Maine.

During this time, he located in Waterville, Me. In July 1892, he resigned and identified himself with the Crystal Water Co., of Edgewater, as superintendent and general manager. Assuming this position with a thorough knowledge of the details of the business, he has been enabled to introduce many valuable reforms, thereby increasing the efficiency of the fire service as well as the domestic supply, and has curtailed the *per capiti* consumption by the introduction of the meters.

Mr. Newhall resides on St. Paul's avenue, Stapleton, with his wife, formerly Miss Annie F. Hubbard, of Oakland, Me., and their twin sons, Guy and Morris, aged four years.

JUSTICE MCGUIRE.

MICHAEL McGUIRE was born in Stapleton in 1861 and was educated at the Broad street public school.

Mr. McGuire is a born politician and an out and out Democrat. He went into politics at an early age and has had a remarkably successful career.

His first office was that of justice of the peace of the town of Middletown, to which he was elected in 1887 when only twenty-six years of age, being at that time one of the youngest justices in the county.

In 1888, he was appointed school collector and was again elected in 1889. In 1890, he was elected town collector and re-elected in 1891.

In the spring of 1892 he was re-elected justice of the peace, and in June of the same year was elected trustee of the village of Edgewater. In 1893, he was elected member of assembly for Richmond county, and in 1894 was re-elected village trustee and now holds the office of village trustee and justice of the peace.

CHARLES E. HOYER.

CHARLES E. HOYER was born March 25th, 1864, only son of the late Captain Chas. W. Hoyer, well known in marine circles, who for many years commanded the famous old Collins Mail Steamship "Atlantic." When a boy, he accompanied his parents at sea and visited nearly every prominent port in the world.

Mr. Hoyer is a graduate of the Broad Street Military Academy at Philadelphia. In 1883, he entered New York journalism and since that time has been the Staten Island correspondent for the leading New York dailies and the Union Press Exchange, representing the New York Associated Press.

In 1892, when a county board of excise was created, Mr. Hoyer was appointed clerk to the new board, which position he now holds for the third consecutive term. He was one of the organizers of the Staten Island Yacht Club, of which organization he for two years was elected commodore. He was also a charter member of Pioneer Lodge No. 335, A. O. U. W., and Stapleton Council No. 1435, Royal Arcanum; was secretary of the former lodge for three years, and is now secretary of the latter lodge. He is also a member of Tompkins Lodge, No. 471 F. & A. M., of Stapleton, the New York Press Club, Staten Island Press Club and an honorably discharged member of the Edgewater Fire Department.

GEORGE W. ELLIS.

Geo. W. Ellis, chief clerk of the Richmond county police department, was born in Woodbridge, N. J., July 28th, 1836. He volunteered in defense of the Union and was appointed quartermaster of the 73rd Regiment of the state of New York and served with that regiment three months. In the year 1869, he was elected supervisor of the town of Westfield. He was elected supervisor in 1870 and was chosen chairman of the board. In 1871, he was appointed unanimously a commissioner of police.

Mr. Ellis has always been a staunch Democrat and an active member of his party. He is a Knight Templar and much interested in Masonic matters.

JAMES SEATON.

JAMES SEATON, the subject of this sketch, was born February 11th, 1868. He is the oldest son of John Seaton, of New Brighton, who has been a justice of the town of Castleton for eight years, and is also grandson of the late James Seaton who has been treasurer of the village of New Brighton for a number of years.

He was educated in district school, No. 3, of Castleton, then took a commercial course in Packard's Business College together with a course in phonography under Prof. James N. Kimball, of that institution, graduating from that institution in 1887.

In December 1890, he was appointed by the board of supervisors as stenographer to District-Attorney Thomas W. Fitzgerald and also stenographer to the grand juries of this county, which positions he now holds, and which enable the grand juries of this county to do more work in a day than ever was accomplished before by the service of a stenographer.

Mr. Seaton is unmarried and lives with his parents at New Brighton.

WM. J. BROWNE.

WM. J. BROWNE was born in New York May 28th, 1858. He came to Staten Island with his parents in 1865 and has since resided here. In 1880, in conjunction with his brother, the late J. H. Browne, he issued the first number of the Richmond County *Democrat*.

On the death of his brother two years ago he became sole proprietor of the paper and has since conducted the same.

HUGO KESSLER.

Hugo Kessler was born in 1849 in Reichenbach, a manufacturing place in Saxony, Germany, at which place his father was a manufacturer of woolen goods. He came to this country in 1867 with his father. He entered the printing business and in a very short time secured a responsible position as foreman of a New York daily.

Later, he was employed for many years on the *Staats-Zeitung*, and in 1883 he established himself in New York under the firm of Meyer & Kessler, which firm to-day is prospering at 91 Cliff street.

Mr. Kessler was married on Staten Island in 1871 to a niece of Capt. Meyer, and since that time, with the exception of a few years, he has been a resident of the Island.

At the urgent requests of many prominent Staten Island Germans, Mr. Kessler established a German newspaper on the Island—the German Staten Island *Post*—in 1888, which paper has rapidly grown and is still increasing in circulation, beside being an excellent advertising medium.

Mr. Kessler is a member of Klopstock Lodge, No. 760, F. & A. M., S. I. Quartette Club, Erheiterung, Turnverein, and also an active member of the Arion Society of New York. He is very popular in German and American social circles.

BENJAMIN E. STREETER.

Proprietor WEST END HOTEL, Tottenville.

This hotel, standing between the Perth Amboy ferry and the Staten Island railroad station, is the most central and conveniently located, as well as the largest, and most commodious hotel in the village.

During the present season Mr. Streeter has built a large new dining-room with kitchen attached. The bar-room, reading-room and restaurant have been refurnished and redecorated, the sleeping-rooms have been furnished in oak, and every part of the hotel has been put in first-class order.

Mr. Streeter's dinners and clam-bakes are known all over the Island, and the hotel is a favorite resort for wheelmen, excursionists and sailing parties.

Benjamin E. Streeter was born in Springfield, Mass., in 1847 and came to Staten Island in 1866 and was for several years conductor on the Staten Island railroad. In 1881, Mr. George Bechtel purcd the West End Hotel from Mr. Nicholas Killmeyer and leased it to Mr. Streeter who had previously had experience in several large city hotels such as the Massasoit House, Springfield, Bagg's Hotel, Utica, and Stanwix Hall, Albany, and has been able to make the West End a success from the beginning.

ANDREW ABRAMS

ANDREWS ABRAMS, architect, carpenter, builder and contractor, Tottenville, was born in Sweden in 1842, and learned his trade in his native town.

At the age of 18 years, he entered the Ancient Marine service and two years later joined the United States Navy, and served on the Virginia, of the Gulf squadron, and assisted in the capture of fifteen blockade runners. At the close of the war he was honorably discharged from the service and settled in Tottenville. He immediately went to work at his trade and soon established himself as a master builder, contractor and architect. Mr. Abrams estimates the number of houses he has built at nearly two hundred, and has built nearly all the houses on Johnson and Wood avenues and Centre street.

His enterprise has kept pace with his industry and he is the owner of eleven houses in Tottenville, most of which are double.

Mr. Abrams is a member of Lenhart Post G. A. R., and one of the trustees of the village of Tottenville.

ELMER E. SLAIGHT.

SLAIGHT & DECKER, grocers, Rossville. Elmer E. Slaight and Alvin S. Decker, both of Rossville, formed a co-partnership in 1891 and began business in the old store occupied for many years by the late Isaac Winant.

Mr. Slaight had been for nine years a clerk in the store of Seguine & Decker at Rossville, where he made a wide acquaintance, which with his personal popularity, had brought a large trade to the firm of Slaight & Decker.

In 1892, they built the large store which they now occupy, corner of Richmond road and Winant avenue. In February 1894, Mr. Slaight was appointed postmaster, the first change in the office in twenty-three years.

Mr. Slaight and Mr. Decker are both members of old Staten Island families, and from the first enjoyed the confidence of the community in which they established their business, and have received a liberal patronage.

T. W. MOORE, JR.

THOMAS WILLIAM MOORE, JR., youngest son of Capt. T. W. Moore, Sr., was born at Annadale in 1870. At the early age of seventeen years he succeeded his father in the grocery business, and a few years later purchased the store and adjoining property.

Mr. Moore is one of the energetic, pushing young men of Staten Island and has succeeded in very largely increasing the business, and now has a trade in groceries, provisions, flour, feed, hay, straw, etc., with customers all the way from New Dorp to Tottenville.

In 1892, he married Miss Gertrude K. Howell, of Huguenot, and has one child, Kitty.

The business was established in 1872 by Capt. T. W. Moore, Sr., who was also a native of Staten Island, and held the office of postmaster for nineteen years, from 1875, until it was removed to the Annadale station in the spring of 1894.

The family have always been staunch Republicans, and have considerable influence in that part of the county.

HORATIO J. SHARRETT.

HORATIO JUDAH SHARRETT was born in Brooklyn in 1870. In 1873, his father moved to West New Brighton, and later, to Port Richmond.

Mr. Sharrett was educated in the Port Richmond High School and was graduated in 1887, at the head of his class and was honored at being chosen its valedictorian.

His first business experience was obtained as clerk in the office of the well-known and popular real estate agent, the late Clarence M. Johnson. On the departure of Mr. Johnson in 1890, for the West, Mr. Sharrett succeeded to the large business of his former employer, and by dint of careful management, energy and liberal advertising, he has succeeded in making for himself a reputation and business as one of the leading real estate agents on the Island.

In 1894, during a hotly contested campaign, Mr. Sharrett was elected town clerk of Northfield on the Republican ticket.

He is a member of different orders and societies, among them the American Legion of Honor, Ancient Order of Foresters, Order of American Firemen, Port Richmond Engine Co., No. 3, and of Trinity M. E. Church.

WILSON A. CLEVELAND.

THERE is no person to whom the village of Garretsons owes more of its rapid growth and prosperity than to Wilson A. Cleveland, architect and builder.

He is a large property owner in the place and has built many of the dwellings there. He also built and owns the block in which the post-office is located, was instrumental in having the post-office established there and was himself appointed postmaster in 1890, an office which he still holds.

Mr. Cleveland was born at Harwich, Mass., May 18th, 1847. On Feb. 28th, 1865, he married Miss Laura J. Watson, daughter of the late Capt. C. H. Watson of the U. S. navy. They have four children, two sons and two daughters.

Mr. Cleveland came to Staten Island in 1872 and his enterprise and thorough knowledge of his trade soon enabled him to take first rank among the builders of Staten Island, and during the twenty-two years that he has lived here, he has worked on many of the finest residences in the county, such as Sir Roderick Cameron's at Arrochar, and David J. Tyson's at Todt Hill. He also superintended the building of Moses Beach's mansion at Peekskill-on-the-Hudson.

EDMUND G. SCHAEFER.

Edmund G. Schaefer, Stapleton, dealer in furniture, and upholstering goods, carpets, oilcloths, etc.

Mr. Schaefer was born in Stapleton in 1869, and was educated in the German Lutheran private school. In 1887, he was made partner with his father in the furniture business, a business which his father had established in 1860. In 1891, he purchased the entire business, and since that time has been sole proprietor. He has been very successful in enlarging the business, and in increasing the patronage of the store, which justly ranks as one of the first and largest of its kind on the Island. Mr. Schaefer has an exceptional business capacity, and is thoroughly conversant with every branch of the trade.

CORNELIUS A. SHEA.

CORNELIUS A. SHEA, cigar manufacturer, Pleasant Plains, was born near Kreischerville in 1845. His father was also a native of Staten Island. His grandfather, William, was one of the most prominent citizens of Rossville and was justice of the peace, notary public, commissioner of deeds and general adviser of the entire community. Shea's lane, now New York avenue, was named in his honor.

In 1870, Mr. Shea was married to Miss Mary E. Cole, daughter of John H. Cole, of Richmond Valley. The same year he opened a cigar factory in the building which he still occupies. He has been clerk of the school district for thirteen years, trustee for nine years, and is now a member of the board of education. He has been trustee of St. Mark's Church for thirteen years and superintendent of the Sunday-school for seventeen years. Mr. Shea has always been an earnest and active Republican but would never accept the nomination for any public office.

MORD'S DRYGOODS EMPORIUM.

A. MORD, Bay street and Vanderbilt avenue, Clifton, dealer in drygoods, clothing, men's furnishing goods, notions, etc.

Mr. Mord established himself in the drygoods and clothing business on Staten Island in 1876, driving his wagon all through the interior of the Island from Clifton to Kreischerville. In 1881, he opened a store at 43 New York avenue, where he conducted business until 1889. He then purchased, at a cost of $12,000, the large store which he now occupies, enlarging and improving it, putting in a glass front, and now has a store 30x60 ft. filled with one of the most complete stocks of drygoods, clothing, etc., to be found on Staten Island. His customers come from every part of the county, and his wagons are out every day delivering goods from St. George to Kreischerville.

Mr. Mord and his sons deserve great credit for the industry and perseverance with which they have pushed their business; and they have had the satisfaction of seeing it grow from a very small beginning to a large and prosperous trade.

CHARLES F. WILBUR.

WILBUR & MANEE, grocers and coal dealers, Pleasant Plains, Prince's Bay P. O.

CHARLES F. WILBUR, senior partner of Wilbur & Manee, was born at Saratoga, New York, in 1854. He came to Staten Island with his father's family in 1857, when his father, John W. Wilbur, came here as contractor for the building of the Staten Island railroad. On the completion of the road, his father was made superintendent, a position which he held, with the exception of a few years, until the opening of the Rapid Transit road in 1886. In 1878, the subject of this sketch was appointed conductor on the railroad, which position he held until his resignation in 1887.

CHARLES C. MANEE.

CHARLES C. MANEE, the junior member of the firm of Wilbur & Manee, is a descendant of one of the old Huguenot families, which settled on Staten Island probably about the close of the seventeenth century. He was born at Pleasant Plains in 1858 and has always resided on the Island. In 1876, he was graduated from the Eastman Business College in Poughkeepsie. In 1888, the firm of Wilbur & Manee was formed and the business of Sebastian LaForge at Pleasant Plains was purchased. Both members of the firm had a wide acquaintance and many personal friends in Westfield, and rapidly built up a large and lucrative business. In 1889, they opened a coal yard, and this branch of the business has also proved successful. The firm has always been known for its fair dealing, and courteous treatment of customers.

STEPHENS HOUSE.

STEPHENS HOUSE, Pleasant Plains, Capt. Stephen H. Slover, proprietor, is one of the best known and best kept road houses in Westfield. It was built by Mr. Slover in 1886 and was the first hotel ever opened in the village.

Capt. Slover is a descendant of the Slover family which settled in the old colonial days. He was born at Old Bridge, Middlesex county, N. J., in 1854, a son of Capt. Joshua Slover. He was graduated from Rutgers College in 1872 when only 18 years of age. He spent the first five years of his business life as clerk in a store and then went into the steamboat business,

STEPHEN H. SLOVER.

and was for ten years captain on the Lehigh Valley Railroad boats plying between Perth Amboy and New York.

In 1883, Mr. Slover married Armenia, daughter of William DeWaters, and granddaughter of the late Abram Latourette. His first hotel venture was as proprietor of the Union hotel, Tottenville. This hotel he kept for two years and during that time he purchased the land and built the hotel which he now occupies. This last venture proved successful beyond his highest hopes, and Mr. Slover is now one of the most prosperous hotel men on the Island.

LEVENGSTON SNEDEKER, JR.

LEVENGSTON SNEDEKER, JR., of Port Richmond, although a young man, is recognized as one of the foremost business men of the north shore. He is engaged in the real estate, general insurance and steamship agency business at the long-established agency of A. Z. Ross, deceased, 133 Richmond terrace, near the Port Richmond post-office, where, although but a short time in business, he has not only kept the bulk of the trade of the old concern, but has largely increased it in volume: this is due to his untiring zeal and activity and to his strictly fair and honest dealings with his patrons.

Among the different reliable and old-established companies for which he is agent, are: Royal, Commercial Union, and Westchester Fire Insurance Companies, New York Life Insurance Company, Travelers' Life and Accident Insurance Company, United States Mutual Accident Association, Lloyd's Plate Glass Insurance Company and the American and White Star steamship lines.

The possession of the above valuable agencies is

a guaranty that any fire or other risks entrusted to him will be placed in first-class companies.

In addition, he is well known and noted as a fine musician and an athlete, being the solo cornetist of the famous Apollo Band of which he is a charter member and was at one time conductor; and is also a member of the athletic corps of the Seventh Regiment, National Guard, New York state. As a musician, he is self-taught; as an athlete, he ranks among the best of amateurs as a runner, having won several prizes in running races, and now holds the championship of the Seventh Regiment.

Mr. Snedeker does not, however, allow any of the above pastimes to interfere with his legitimate business.

As a further mark of the esteem and confidence in which Mr. Snedeker is held, the Co-operative Building Bank of New York has selected him as its representative in Port Richmond, where he has established a branch of the parent company.

All persons having any business in his line, may feel assured that, if entrusted to him, it will receive prompt and careful attention.

Mr. Snedeker was born in Elizabeth, N. J., twenty-three years ago, but when about five months old, with his parents, he came to Staten Island, where he has since resided and become identified with its interests. By marriage he is connected with the old Van-Duzer family whose ancestors for generations were born on Staten Island, and on his mother's side he is related to the Vanderbilt family, thereby more closely allying himself to Richmond county.

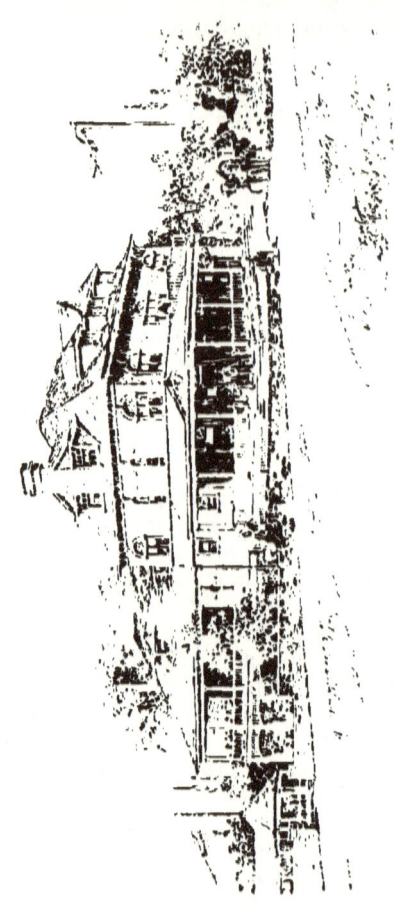

ATLANTIC INN, GARRETSONS, STATEN ISLAND.
Erected 1893.

THE ATLANTIC INN.

THE ATLANTIC INN, Grant City, E. C. Werthmuller, proprietor, is one of the largest and finest new roadhouses on Staten Island, and is a favorite stopping-place for the members of the L. A. W., for family parties, driving parties, etc. It has wide shady verandas, elegant rooms handsomely furnished, and its bar and table are always supplied with the best the season affords. The proprietor spares no pains to make his guests comfortable and to supply them with everything they may desire.

The hotel is also provided with ample sheds and stables for the horses and carriages of both permanent and transient guests.

The hotel stands in a healthful location and commands a magnificent view of the bay from Sandy Hook to Coney Island, and is the nearest point to the Vanderbilt mausoleum, said to be the handsomest and most costly tomb in the world.

FRED WILKINS.

FRED WILKINS, proprietor of the Oriental Hotel and Oriental Park Hotel, may well be called the founder of Eltingville. When he located there twenty-eight years ago, there were but two houses in the village.

He purchased a plot of two and a half acres of swamp land adjoining Eltingville station, drained it and filled it in, and with his own hands planted the trees which now form what is probably the finest grove and picnic grounds on Staten Island, and in 1874 he built the Oriental Hotel.

When he planted the grove, looking forward to the time when it would become a favorite resort for picnic parties and clubs from New York, his friends remarked that he would never be able to compete with the parks and play-grounds of New York for popular favor, but he replied that by the time his trees were grown picnic parties in the New York parks would be a thing of the past. Time has proved Mr. Wilkins' prophecy to be correct and fully justified his enterprise and farsightedness in expending the large sums of money required to redeem the swamp and make it a delightful summer resort.

In 1876, Mr. Wilkins built in the centre of the grove what at that time was the largest and finest dancing pavilion on Staten Island, with bowling alley, shooting gallery, etc., attached.

In the spring of 1894, he rebuilt the old grocery on the corner of Amboy avenue and Eltingville avenue, and transformed it into the Oriental Park Hotel, one of the finest road-houses in the county.

Mr. Wilkins has always had great faith in the future of Staten Island and has spent his money liberally to improve and beautify his property.

MARSENA COUNSELLOR AYRES.

MARSENA COUNSELLOR AYRES, harness-maker, Richmond Valley (Tottenville P. O.), keeps a full line of robes, blankets and all kinds of horse furnishings. The business was originally established in 1861 by his father, the late Michael C. Ayres, previously of Rahway, N. J. The business has been continued in this same location for thirty-two years; from 1861 to 1871 by the late Michael C. Ayres, from 1869 to 1886 by Mr. Ayres and his son, the present proprietor, and since that time by the latter. Mr. M. C. Ayres, the founder of the business, was, during his lifetime, one of the best known and best respected men of Tottenville. He was for over twenty years clerk of the South Baptist Church, and for several years was a member of the board of town auditors and took an active part in all matters pertaining to the welfare of the general community. His death occurred in 1886 and was a great loss not only to the South Baptist Church, but to the entire community.

THE LATE MICHAEL C. AYRES.

JAMES D. KEELEY.

JAMES D. KEELEY, town clerk of the town of Southfield, was born Aug. 20th, 1868, is a native of Clifton and son of Daniel Keeley, ex-supervisor of the town of Southfield. He was educated in the public schools of Staten Island, and is a solid Democrat. Mr. Keeley is a builder by trade, and is one of the prominent builders of Southfield, where he has built a number of handsome buildings.

He also holds the office of school collector of his district, and was elected town clerk at the last election. He has the distinction of being the youngest man ever elected to the office which he now holds.

ISRAEL BUTLER, JR.

BUTLER BROS., architects, contractors, carpenters and builders, Tottenville. This firm consists of Israel Butler, Jr., and David J. Butler, and was established in 1889.

The first building erected by the firm was the residence of ex-Sheriff Vaughan on Fisher avenue, Tottenville. From the first this firm has been one of the leading of Westfield and has put up some of the largest and finest buildings in the town, among which we may note the large residences of Richard Berg, at Annadale; Arthur W. Browne and George L. Harrison, at Pleasant Plains; R. C. Watson, H. S. Bedell and Geo. Cunning-

DAVID J. BUTLER.

ham at Tottenville; and Claus Wilkins at Kreischerville.

This firm also built the large hotels of Christian Nielson and Mrs. Lorretta Killmeyer at Kreischerville, Amicitia Hall at Pleasant Plains, the Aquehonga clubhouse at Tottenville, and Elmer T. Butler's coach house and stables on the south shore.

Both members of the firm are young and enterprising men, sons of the late Israel Butler, Sr., who was a prominent builder in the earlier days of Tottenville, and bid fair to do their part to building up the west side of the Island.

JACOB S. ELLIS.

Jacob S. Ellis & Son, ship and boat builders, Tottenville.

Jacob S. Ellis was born near Rossville, in 1820, was brought up and educated on Staten Island and learned his trade in Webb's shipyard in New York. In 1850, he located at Belleville, N. J., where he carried on the business of building freight schooners until 1861, when Mr. Ellis returned to Staten Island and purchased the shipyard now owned by J. S. Ellis & Son, and where for over thirty years he has carried on a large and successful business.

Hampton C. Ellis, the junior member of the firm, was born in Belleville, N. J., in 1860, while his father was in business at that place. He was reared and

HAMPTON C. ELLIS.

educated on Staten Island, and at the age of twenty-one years was taken into partnership with his father.

Among the vessels which they have built and which are still in service are the following: Pilot boats, Thos. D. Harrison, Jos. F. Loubat, Wm. H. Starbuck; tugs, Chas. Runyan, Rambler, E. E. Heipershausen, Jos. Peene. Jr., D. S. Asnot; brigs, Nettie, Robert Dillon; bark, John Zittolosen; schooners, Luola Merchison, E. S. Porrel, Sunny South, Harry Knowlton, Asa Lyons, Oliver Schofield, Helen A. Hoyt.

The firm have always enjoyed an excellent reputation, not only for honesty and responsibility, but for skill and designing vessels, and promptness and enterprise with which their contracts are executed.

JUSTICE WOOD.

JUSTICE WOOD.

John B. Wood, justice of the peace of the town of Westfield, was born in Perth Amboy, N. J., in 1840, son of the late Joseph B. Wood. Although born in New Jersey Mr. Wood comes of a long line of ancestors who have been prominent in the official and business life of Staten Island.

After obtaining a thorough public school education, Mr. Wood learned the trade of ship-carpenter with his uncle, after which he learned the trade of steam-heating and gas-fitting under John W. Sneath, engineer of the well-known firm of Mason & Dodge, of New York, pioneers in the steam-heating business.

Mr. Wood was for a long time employed on steam-heaters for the Jewett oil-cloth factory, at Elizabethport, N. J., and helped to fit up P. T. Barnum's old museum, and was for years superintendent of the steam-heating machinery department of Stewart Greer & Co., sugar refiners, of New York. He was also the first engineer employed at the Sayre & Fisher fire-brick factory at Sayreville, N. J., and in 1890 designed and superintended the building of O. H. Barnard's silk mill at Richmond Valley, put in the engine, boiler, gas plant and all the machinery.

In 1872, Mr. Wood moved to Tottenville, and two years later was appointed justice of the peace to fill a vacancy, and was twice elected on the Republican ticket and held the office for eight years. He was again appointed to fill a vacancy in 1894, caused by the death of Justice C. H. Pendexter, which office he still holds.

Mr. Wood is a master mason in good standing and is president of the Westfield branch of the New York Mutual Loan and Savings Association.

HOWARD M. VERE, D. D. S.

Howard M. Vere, D. D. S., was born in New York city, but came to Staten Island with his father's family when a young lad. He was educated in the best schools of Staten Island, finishing at D. L. Moody's academy, Mt. Hermon, Mass. After the completion of his academic course, he entered his father's dental office at West New Brighton, where he studied four years.

In 1890, he entered the New York College of Dentistry, from which he was graduated with honor in 1892. He then returned to Staten Island, and entered into partnership with his father, Dr. J. H. Vere, one of the best known dentists of the Island.

This firm enjoy the patronage of the community and a large and lucrative practice, patients coming from all parts of the Island, beside a first-class clientage from New York city. Their practice is constantly growing and no dentists on the Island have a better reputation for first-class work than this firm.

JACOB HERREL.

JACOB HERREL, dealer in boots and shoes and rubber goods, Tottenville, opened the first shoe store ever kept in the village of Tottenville.

Mr. Herrel was born in Baden, Germany, in 1833 and in 1850 he came to America and settled at Port Jervis, N. Y., where he learned the shoemaker's trade. He came to Staten Island in 1856 and opened a custom shoe shop. In 1862, he built a store on Main street which he has since occupied and which was, until a few years ago, the only exclusive shoe store on this end of the Island.

Mr. Herrel was trustee of the village for several years under the revived charter, and has been trustee of the public school for many years, an office which he now holds.

He was married in 1859 to Miss Katherine Seeger of Wurtemberg, Germany, who died in 1891. He has six children: George, Kate, Emma, Louise, William J. and Sophia (Mrs. Henry Lindenmeyer, of New York.)

H. E. CLEVELAND.

H. E. CLEVELAND.

HENRY E. CLEVELAND came of a long line of ancestors (English) who settled in the wilds of central Massachusetts on the border line of the Pequod country, about the middle of the eighteenth century. They were among the sturdy pioneers who helped to clear up the country, to establish schools, academies and colleges and push forward the cause of civilization, in the days when the pine knot furnished the "electric" midnight light of the student for poring over the pages of Virgil and solving the propositions of Euclid.

Under such circumstances, was developed the class of men dubbed the "schoolmasters abroad."

As one of this class Mr. Cleveland came to Clifton, where he taught three successive generations of scholars, having for associates such faithful and efficient co-workers as Messrs. Wright, Sprague, Annan, Hervey, Blen, etc., and for school commissioner for a series of years the "noblest Roman of them all," the Rev. Dr. Brownlee.

Mr. Cleveland bears the proud distinction of having taught in the same public school for more successive years than any other teacher in the state, and he has seen many of his scholars enter almost every walk of industrial, professional and official life and has the satisfaction of knowing that many men owe their success to his instruction.

Mr. Cleveland has retired from teaching and is living quietly at Garretsons looking after the property which he has accumulated by a long life of industry.

PHILLIP J. BROWN.

PHILLIP J. BROWN.

Phillip J. Brown was born in Rahway, N. J., Feb. 7th, 1839. At the age of seventeen years, he went to learn the carriage trade, and four years later, having learned what he could in his native town, he went to New Haven with the firm of Lawrence, Bradley & Co., the noted carriage builders, and a short time afterward he came to New York with the firm of J. B. Brewster & Co., of Twenty-fifth street, one of the most celebrated firms of carriage builders in the world. He remained here six years, thoroughly mastering the carriage trade. He then returned to his native city, where he started in the carriage business for himself, and continued (with many ups and downs), until the fall of 1871, when a fire destroyed his shop and everything in it except a few finished carriages.

In 1872, he came to Staten Island, and two years later he again established himself in business, and by building nothing but first-class carriages soon established for himself an excellent reputation and found ready sale for his work, not only among the best people of Staten Island but in Bayonne, New York and Brooklyn, and his work stands to-day at the head of the carriage trade on Staten Island.

Mr. Brown does his own drafting and all his work is made under his own careful supervision.

In 1884, Mr. Brown started a livery stable on a small scale, increasing his stock year by year, until he now has the best-equipped stable on Staten Island, with special facilities, and experienced men for moving pianos and furniture. He also has extensive furniture warehouses, covered furniture vans, etc.

In 1890, Mr. Brown opened a repository with as fine a display of carriages, wagons, harness and horse clothing, as was ever opened on the Island.

PETER FLOERSCH.

PETER FLOERSCH, proprietor of the Excelsior Hotel, Main street, Tottenville, was born in Germany on the Rhine in 1860, and when only four years of age, came to this country with his father's family, who settled in Newark, N. J. He came to Staten Island in 1874, and in 1877 settled in Tottenville, and opened a barber shop in Nelson's Hotel, four years later. In 1886, he leased the Sevenhaar block and opened the Excelsior Hotel, with restaurant and billiard-room attached, where he has since done a very successful business. For two years he was lessee of the Bay Cliff Park restaurant.

Mr. Floersch has always been a prominent and active Republican and has assisted his party through a great many hot campaigns. He was elected excise commissioner on the Republican ticket and served three years.

JOHN T. FURMAN.

JOHN T. FURMAN, contractor and road builder, was born at Newtown, L. I., in 1840. He was brought up and educated in Newtown and when he came of age he established himself in business as general contractor and road-builder, etc. He came to Staten Island in 1881 and is now serving his second term as highway commissioner. The most important road improvements have been carried out under his supervision. He has also executed a large number of contracts for opening up Staten Island property for settlement, among which were the laying out and grading of the Barclay property at Annadale, and the Wiman property at Fox Hill, Clifton.

Mr. Furman's work has always been noted for the thoroughness and honesty with which he carries out his contracts.

NICHOLAS KILLMEYER.

Nicholas Killmeyer, Kreischerville grocer, and proprietor of the Union Hotel, Kreischerville, was born in Prussia in 1822. He came to America in 1849 and settled in Woodbridge, N. J. In 1850, he came to Kreischerville and was in the employ of B. Kreischer & Co. until 1863. In 1859, he built a hotel and grocery on the ground now occupied by the Union Hotel, and in 1873 he built the store which he now occupies. In 1890, he enlarged and refurnished his hotel, and now has probably the handsomest bar and billiard rooms on the Island.

In 1879, Mr. Killmeyer and his eldest son, William, bought the West End Hotel, Tottenville, and it was conducted by William until 1886, when they sold the property to the late George Bechtel.

Mr. Killmeyer has conducted the largest business of anyone in Kreischerville, and his grocery and hotel have always been the principal store and house of entertainment.

In 1863, the first post-office was established in Kreischerville, and Mr. Killmeyer was appointed postmaster. He held the office for thirteen years, when political influence caused the office to be discontinued, but it was re-established in 1886 and Mr. Killmeyer's son Albert was appointed to the office, which he held until 1892.

Mr. Killmeyer has now practically retired from business and has turned over the management of his store to his son Albert, and his hotel to his son Theodore.

Mr. Killmeyer was the father of seven children: Four sons, William, Henry, (deceased), August, (deceased), Albert and Theodore, and two daughters, Lena, (Mrs. W. G. Underhill, of Perth Amboy), and Katie (Mrs. J. E. Dailey), of Brooklyn.

DAVID C. BUTLER.

DAVID C. BUTLER, ship-builder, Ward's Point, Tottenville, was born in Tottenville in 1834. His father, the late Henry Butler, was also a native of Staten Island, and served in the militia in the war of 1812. At the age of seventeen he went to work in the shipyard of David Crowell at Perth Amboy, N. J., and learned his trade, after which he worked in Keyport, N. J., until 1863. He then returned to Tottenville and purchased from his brother James a one-half interest in the Ward's Point shipyard. A few years later he bought his brother's entire interest and from that time has done a large and successful business of repairing, overhauling and rebuilding vessels from all parts of the country.

Mr. Butler has also found time during his busy career to take an active interest in matters pertaining to the public welfare, and it is largely due to his influence and energy that Tottenville is indebted for the present handsome and commodious public school building, which at the time of its erection, was one of the largest on the Island.

St. Paul's Church is also indebted to Mr. Butler for its present capacious Sunday-school room. In 1884, when Mr. Butler found that the Sunday-school had entirely outgrown its accommodations, and as the trustees of the church were unwilling to resume the responsibility of enlarging the Sunday-school room, Mr. Butler offered, if they would give him permission, to have the work done and he would assume the responsibity for the entire cost of the improvement. After much hesitation and delay, the trustees gave their consent, upon Mr. Butler giving his personal bond to meet all charges of the new building. The work was completed in due time and Mr. Butler redeemed all his pledges.

Mr. Butler was for three years secretary of the Richmond County Sunday-school Association (nonsectarian), and is a member of the board for the establishment of the Richmond County Bible Society.

Mr. Butler is a Democrat and he has had offered him on several occasions several of the best offices the county affords. He postively refused all offers because he felt it would effect him in his church work which he so much loved and enjoyed, and as he stood before the school as their superintendent for over twenty years he did not wish to take any political office for fear it might effect his influence spiritually with his Sunday-school.

GEORGE L. EGBERT.

About George L. Egbert we need say little, as he is such an extensive advertiser that he is well known to Staten Islanders.

Mr. Egbert was born at Port Richmond in 1862, and after receiving a common school education, embarked as a clerk, in the retail business, at the age of seventeen years.

At the expiration of ten years, he ended his clerkship and in 1879 started in business under his own name, at Tompkinsville. He began business on a small scale, gradually increasing it, until now his store, devoted to men's furnishing goods, is one of the largest in the county.

Mr. Egbert is interested in every movement for the development of Staten Island. He is a member of numerous organizations.

E. STEWART MANEE.

E. STEWART MANEE, president of the village of Tottenville, is the elder son of Elias P. Manee and the late Margaretta Stewart.

He was born in Tottenville in 1866. His paternal ancestors were Huguenots who settled on Staten Island 200 years ago. His mother was born in London.

He is a graduate of the local school and of Packard's Business College and occupies a responsible position in the marine insurance office of United States "Lloyds," by whom he has been employed for more than ten years. He is a member of St. Paul's M. E. Church, and is a Republican in politics.

In November 1893, he married Amanda, elder daughter of William Britton, of New York city.

Mr. Manee has a keen appreciation of the natural beauties and possibilities of Staten Island and has been largely instrumental in securing a village government for Tottenville and hopes soon to see that pretty suburb modernized.

DR. S. J. KENNEDY.

Dr. S. J. Kennedy, dentist, New Dorp, was born in Illinois in 1866. He came to New York with his father's family when only two years of age, and was brought up and educated in New York city. He was graduated from the College of the City of New York in 1881. After his graduation, he entered the dental office of his father, Dr. John C. Kennedy, and two years later entered the New York College of Dentistry, from which he was graduated at the age of twenty-one years, the youngest graduate in his class. After graduating, he returned to his father's office, where he still continues in practice. In 1891, the family moved to New Dorp, where the doctor opened a branch of his New York Dental rooms, and has built up a large and constantly growing practice.

Dr. Kennedy is one of the few professional men who always study their profession as well as practice it; and he has kept abreast of all the recent improvements in dental surgery, and is reckoned by his patients as one of the most careful and skillful dentists on Staten Island.

WILLIAM. TYSEN.

WILLIAM TYSEN, architect, carpenter and builder, is one of the prominent builders of the west end of Staten Island. He is a Staten Islander by birth and a lineal descendant of Barne Tysen who settled on the Island in the old colonial days. Mr. Tysen was educated in the Staten Island public schools, and at the age of twenty-one he went to learn the trade of carpenter and builder.

Before entering into business for himself he worked as journeyman and foreman for some of the best builders on the Island and acquired thorough knowledge of the business. In 1886, he established himself in business and located in Tottenville, where he has won a reputation for fair dealing and good honest work.

Barne Tysen, the first of the Tysens on Staten Island, came from Amsterdam in 1660 and obtained a grant of land from Andros in 1677 and built the stone house known for generations as the Barne Tysen house. The family have been prominent in church and official circles, having served faithfully in both Congress and the state Legislature, and in the judicatory.

JAMES LA FORGE.

James LaForge, collector of taxes for the town of Westfield, was born at Pleasant Plains in 1848, and was brought up and educated in the same village. His first business venture was as oyster planter, a business which he carried on successfully for over twenty years. In the spring of 1892, he was elected collector on the Republican ticket for the town of Westfield, defeating Sidney Post, the Democratic nominee, by a majority of 200. He was re-elected in 1893 and again in 1894, both years without any opposition. This was an indorsement as remarkable as it was emphatic, for the office had previously been held by the Democrats for sixteen successive years, with the exception of one year, and yet Mr. LaForge was unanimously elected to the best-paying office of the town, for two successive years.

In 1892, Mr. LaForge engaged in the flour and feed business, which he has pushed with such success that he now probably sells nearly as much flour, feed and hay, especially the latter two, as all the other dealers in the town combined.

In addition, Mr. LaForge does a considerable real estate business. In 1888, he purchased the property known as the Excelsior base-ball grounds, consisting of twelve acres on Bayview avenue, the best-located property in the vicinity. He laid this property out and improved it and has sold a number of lots on which handsome residences have already been erected.

Altogether, Mr. LaForge is one of the most popular officials and enterprising men of the town of Westfield.

WILLIAM H. TOTTEN.

WILLIAM H. TOTTEN, grocer, Main street, Tottenville, is one of the oldest business men of this end of the Island. He was born in 1825. His father, Capt. John Totten, was one of the original settlers and may be regarded as the founder of Tottenville. He built the first dock in the village and opened the first store. At his death, in 1866, he was succeeded by his son, the subject of this sketch, who has all his life, been engaged in business in Tottenville, and is now doing a successful grocery business.

S. D. SIMONSON & CO.

This firm was organized January 1st, 1893, for the purpose of transacting a general real estate and fire insurance agency and brokerage business in the city of New York and in Richmond county, and succeeded to the business of the old firm of Miller & Simonson.

The senior member of the firm, Mr. Stephen D. Simonson, was for many years connected with the New York City Fire Insurance Company, and in January 1877 organized with Mr. Howard R. Miller the firm of Miller & Simonson, which transacted for sixteen years a large and successful real estate and fire insurance business in New York and on Staten Island.

Mr. John Frederick Smith, the junior member, began his business career in New York with Messrs. A. A. French & Co., manufacturers of fishermen's supplies, and in February 1877, entered the employ of Messrs. Miller & Simonson and afterward became manager of the Staten Island office.

The main offices of the firm are at 46 Cedar street, New York, and 177 Richmond terrace, West New Brighton, with branch offices at New Brighton, Tompkinsville, Stapleton and Port Richmond.

They are intrusted with the full care and management of a very large amount of valuable property, and have been successful in selling a large amount of Staten Island property. They are also the general agents for Staten Island of the Liverpool, London and Globe, Aetna of Hartford, Continental, Hanover and German-American of New York, Phenix of Brooklyn, and Glens Falls Fire Insurance Companies, also New York Plate Glass Insurance Company.

WALTER MARSHALL.

WALTER MARSHALL, hardware dealer, Prince's Bay. Builders' hardware, cutlery, carpenters' tools, house-furnishing hardware, etc.

Mr. Marshall was born and educated on Staten Island, and in 1889 established the first exclusively hardware store ever kept in the town of Westfield. Considerable doubt was felt at the time whether such a business would pay, in view of the fact that a number of grocers kept small stocks of hardware. In spite of all doubts, however, the business has been fairly successful from the beginning.

In March 1894, Mr. Marshall was appointed postmaster, which office he still holds.

Residence of CROWELL M SEGUINE, Giffords-by-the-Sea, Staten Island.

J. KADLETZ.

J. KADLETZ, florist and horticulturist, Garretson, was born at Prague, Austria, and is a graduate of the University of Prague, founded in 1348, the oldest college in central Europe. Mr. Kadletz learned the business of florist in his native city and learned it thoroughly, as men of the old world are wont to learn anything they undertake.

He came to America and settled on Staten Island in 1856 and established himself in the florist's business at Garretsons. In 1865, he purchased the property now occupied by his extensive gardens and greenhouses at the corner of Richmond road and Sea View avenue, where he cultivates a large variety of plants and shrubs of all kinds.

Mr. Kadletz's favorite flower and the one to which he gives his special attention is the rose, and of this he has not only all the kinds usually grown in the flower garden, but also many new and rare varieties.

Mr. Kadletz, in addition to his excellent business abilities, is a man of unusual culture, and is not only a fine classical scholar but is also thoroughly familiar with the best literature of the day, which he is able to read not only in English and Austrian, but in German as well.

JAMES FOSTER.

JAMES FOSTER, nurseryman, Eltingville, (Sea Side P. O.), was born in the city of Lincolnshire, England. He came to America in 1848. In 1860, he established himself in the nursery business, near Eltingville, which he has carried on successfully up to the present time. There is probably no man on Staten Island who has a more thorough knowledge of the business, especially in its relation to the soil and climate of Staten Island, than Mr. Foster, and in his nurseries at Eltingville he has not only a great variety of flowering plants, both annual and hardy, but all kinds of ornamental fruit and shade trees adapted to our climate. His long experience in the business has given him a thorough knowledge how to produce the best results in landscape gardening.

Those who have seen the wonderful growth of the plants and vines at the Vanderbilt mausoleum and the beautiful effects produced show that Mr. Foster thoroughly understands his business.

Mr. Foster has planted many ornamental trees on the Vanderbilt homestead and many of the finest trees on the streets of New Dorp, Oakwood, etc., a large number which were used to replace trees furnished by other nurserymen, and which had either died or failed to give satisfactory results.

Mr. Foster always has in his nursery a large stock and is prepared to fill orders large or small on short notice and to guarantee satisfactory results.

JAMES MCCABE.

JAMES MCCABE, of the firm of McCabe Bros., proprietors of the Greenridge brick-yards, was born at Haverstraw, N. Y., in 1861 and was educated in the best schools of that village. In 1881, he and his brother John came to Staten Island and under the firm name and style of McCabe Bros., leased the old Bennett brick-yard at Fresh Kills and engaged in the manufacture of building brick. The venture proved successful, so much so that in 1889, they purchased the entire plant and property and the next year put in steam power. Under their management the capacity of their works has been increased from 5,000,000 to 10,000,000 bricks per year.

In addition to giving his personal attention to the large business interests of McCabe Bros., Mr. McCabe has kept up his studies in science and the classics and was graduated from Manhattan college in 1882 with the degree of A. B. In 1889, he was graduated from the Columbia law school with the degree of L. L. B. and was admitted to the bar in the same year.

Mr. McCabe has often been urged to take the nomination on the Democratic ticket for the highest offices in the town, but, with the exception of one term, which he served as highway commissioner, he has refused to accept any office.